M000204727

Croatia

by Tony Kelly

Tony Kelly first visited Croatia in the 1980s when it was still part of Yugoslavia and returned 20 years later to find a confident, independent country. A prolific writer on Spain, his other guidebooks include *AA Essential Mallorca, Menorca* and *Costa Brava*, and Spiral Guides to Gran Canaria and Portugal.

Above: *rooftop view of Rovinj's harbour*

AA Publishing

Zlatni Rat, near Bol

First published 2006.

© Automobile Association Developments Limited 2006.

Published by AA Publishing, a trading name of Automobile Association Developments Limited, whose registered office is Fanum House, Basing View, Basingstoke, Hampshire RG21 4EA. Registered number 1878835

Find out more about AA Publishing and the wide range of travel publications and services the AA provides by visiting our website at www.theAA.com/bookshop

Colour separation: Keenes, Andover
Printed and bound in Italy by Printer Trento S.r.l

A02345
Maps produced from data supplied by Global Mapping, Brackley, UK. Copyright © Global Mapping/Hibernia

Contents

About this Book

This book is divided into five sections to cover the most important aspects of your visit to Croatia.

Viewing Croatia pages 5–14
An introduction to Croatia by the author.
Croatia's Features
Essence of Croatia
The Shaping of Croatia
Peace and Quiet
Croatia's Famous

Top Ten pages 15–26
The author's choice of the Top Ten places to see in Croatia, listed in alphabetical order, each with practical information.

What to See pages 27–90
Three sections: Inland Croatia, Istria and Kvarner and Dalmatia, each with its own brief introduction and an alphabetical listing of the main attractions.
Practical information
Snippets of 'Did you know...' information
4 suggested walks
4 suggested tours
2 features

Where To... pages 91–116
Detailed listings of the best places to eat, stay, shop, take the children and be entertained.

4

Practical Matters pages 117–124
A highly visual section containing essential travel information.

Maps
All map references are to the individual maps found in the What to See section of this guide.
For example, the Pula Arena has the reference ✚ 56 A1 – indicating the page on which the map is located and the grid square in which the arena is to be found. A list of the maps that have been used in this travel guide can be found in the index.

Prices
Where appropriate, an indication of the cost of an establishment is given by € signs:
€€€ denotes higher prices, €€ denotes average prices, while € denotes lower charges.

Star Ratings
Most of the places described in this book have been given a separate rating:

✪✪✪   Do not miss
✪✪   Highly recommended
✪   Worth seeing

Viewing
Croatia

Above: view from the road between
Bol and Murvica
Right: Tomislav, Croatia's first king, in the
square named after him in Zagreb

5

Tony Kelly's Croatia

Croatia's Neighbours
Croatia is one of five countries to have emerged from the break-up of the former Yugoslavia. The others are Bosnia-Herzegovina, Macedonia, Slovenia and the republic of Serbia and Montenegro. Croatia shares land borders with all of these except for Macedonia, and with Hungary. It also shares a sea border with Italy, which faces Croatia across the Adriatic.

The harbour promenade at Rovinj

It has more than a thousand islands, a beautiful coastline and the cleanest waters in the Mediterranean. It has mountains, lakes, waterfalls, rivers, buzzing cities and historic Venetian towns. In short, it has everything you could want for a perfect holiday. So why aren't more people discovering Croatia?

Before 1990, crowds flocked to the Adriatic beaches of what was then part of Yugoslavia. Then along came the wars that tore Yugoslavia apart, and Croatia disappeared off the tourist map. The majority of the coastal resorts were unaffected by the fighting but people saw a country at war and stayed away.

Ten years after the end of the war, Croatia is welcoming tourists again. The country is safe to visit and there are few visible signs of damage, unless you venture inland to the border areas of Slavonia and Dalmatia. Forced to rebuild its tourist industry from scratch, Croatia has learned from the mistakes of the past. Golf courses, marinas and cycle routes are being developed; the new trends are towards rural tourism and small family-run hotels as Croatia rejects 'hamburgerisation' and embraces a future that puts quality before quantity.

Croatia is fast becoming the hottest destination in the Med, with royalty and film stars regularly dropping by on their yachts. Journalists have christened it the New Tuscany and the New Greece. But Croatia does not need such comparisons for its charms to be appreciated. This is a young, confident country, taking its place in modern Europe. Go now to experience the New Croatia.

Croatia's Features

People
- Croatia has a population of just under 4.5 million people, according to a census carried out in 2001.
- Zagreb, the capital, has a population of almost a million. The next biggest cities are Split, Rijeka, Osijek and Zadar.
- Around 90 per cent of the population are ethnic Croats and 5 per cent are Serbs.
- Religion is divided along ethnic lines, with 88 per cent being Roman Catholic and 4 per cent Serbian Orthodox.
- Around 40 per cent of Croatians had access to the internet at the start of 2005.

View across to the island of Korčula

Geography
- Croatia has 5,835km (3,618 miles) of coastline, of which 4,058km (2,516 miles) is on islands and 1,777km (1,102 miles) on the mainland.
- There are 1,185 islands, of which about 50 are inhabited.
- The highest mountain is Dinara (1,831m/5,987ft), on the Bosnian border near Knin.
- The longest river is the Sava, which runs for 562km (348 miles) across Croatia. Other major rivers are the Drava and the Danube, which form the borders with Hungary and Serbia.

The Croatian Flag
Croatia's flag, adopted in 1991, is a red, white and blue tricolour arranged in horizontal lines with a coat of arms at the centre. This features the traditional red-and-white chequerboard, crowned by five shields representing the historic coats of arms of Croatia, Dubrovnik, Dalmatia, Istria and Slavonia.

Tourism
- Croatia received almost 8 million foreign tourists in 2004. Of these, 20 per cent were from Germany and 15 per cent from Italy, followed by Slovenia, Austria, the Czech Republic and Hungary.
- Istria is the most popular region, receiving 2.5 million foreign tourists in 2004.
- The number of British visitors reached 470,000 in 1990 but by 2004 it had only recovered to 208,000.

Essence of Croatia

Tourists taking it easy in Poreč (below) and Dubrovnik (bottom)

From the eastern plains of Slavonia to the fashionable Adriatic coast, Croatia is a fascinating blend of Balkan, central European and Mediterranean cultures. This is a country which has taken on influences from Venice to Vienna and Belgrade to Istanbul, and moulded them to create a distinct national character. The people of Croatia are patriotic but welcoming to strangers, proud of their history yet open to new ideas. Despite the traumas of their recent past, they have a relaxed Mediterranean attitude to life and like nothing better than to sit outside a café with friends.

THE **10** ESSENTIALS

If you only have a short time to visit Croatia, or would like to get a really complete picture of the country, here are the essentials:

Left: view from the campanile in Rovinj

Below: making the most of the sun on Zlatni Rat beach, near Bol

• **Take a walk around Dubrovnik's city walls,** then plunge into the medieval streets of the old town, with its beautifully restored churches, fountains and palaces (► 16).

• **Go island-hopping in the Adriatic** using the excellent network of ferries—better still, hire your own yacht (► 115).

• **Spend a day admiring the scenery of the Plitvice Lakes** (► 21) or Krka National Park (► 83), with their stunning emerald-green waterfalls, rivers and lakes.

• **Sample fresh truffles in the hill towns of inland Istria** (► 59), then head down to the coast for an evening by the sea in pretty-as-a-picture Rovinj (► 23).

• **Play gladiators in the Roman arena at Pula** (► 22)—if you can, go to a concert here.

• **Have coffee in Trg Bana Jelačića in Zagreb** (► 40), then take the funicular to Gornji Grad (► 18) to explore the oldest part of the city.

• **Soak up the laid-back atmosphere** and baroque architecture of Croatia's inland towns such as Varaždin (► 25) and Samobor (► 49).

• **Take in a performance** during one of the summer festivals in Dubrovnik, Split and towns along the coast (► 86).

• **Sip chilled *prošek* or malvazija wine** on a summer evening by the sea, then dine on simply grilled fresh fish at a harbourside restaurant.

• **Take off all your clothes** and dress as nature intended on one of Croatia's nudist beaches—everyone else does it, and you will never get a better chance.

The Shaping of Croatia

Celebrating Nazi defeat

Around 30,000 BC
First evidence of human habitation, with the discovery of Krapina Man in caves near Zagreb.

6th century BC
The Greeks establish trading colonies at Pharos (Hvar), Issa (Vis), Korčula, Trogir and Cavtat, living alongside native Illyrian tribes.

1st century BC
The Romans conquer Croatia and establish the provinces of Dalmatia and Pannonia.

AD 305
Completion of Roman emperor Diocletian's palace at Split.

395
The Roman empire is divided into eastern and western spheres, creating a boundary between Catholic and Orthodox along the border of modern-day Croatia and Serbia.

7th century
Slav tribes from Poland and Ukraine migrate to the Balkans. A group known as Croats settles in Slavonia and Dalmatia.

925
Tomislav becomes the first king of Croatia.

1089
Death of Zvonimir, the last king of Croatia.

1094
Founding of Zagreb.

1102
Croatia enters a union with Hungary, under the Hungarian monarchy but with its own *ban* (governor) and *sabor* (parliament).

14th century
The rise of Venetian power sees Venice control most of Dalmatia, except for Dubrovnik, which becomes the republic of Ragusa.

1527
Croatia passes to the Hapsburg (Austro-Hungarian) dynasty. Constant battles between Hapsburg and Ottoman forces lead to the construction of the

Vojna Krajina (Military Frontier) along the border with present-day Bosnia. Serbs are encouraged to settle in the Krajina region to form a defensive army against the Ottoman Turks.

1667
An earthquake destroys much of Dubrovnik.

1809
The French emperor Napoleon captures Dalmatia and rules it as the Illyrian Provinces.

1815
The Congress of Vienna awards Dalmatia to the Hapsburg empire, uniting Croatia under Austro-Hungarian rule.

1918
Following World War I and the collapse of the Hapsburg monarchy, Croatia enters the

Kingdom of Serbs, Croats and Slovenes, later renamed Yugoslavia. Istria becomes part of Italy until 1945.

1941–5
German and Italian forces occupy Croatia and establish a Nazi puppet state known as the Ustaše, which carries out atrocities and murders of ethnic Serbs. Tito organizes Partisan resistance throughout Yugoslavia with the support of Allied forces from Britain.

1945–80
Yugoslavia is re-established as a

President Tuđman

Fighting at Knin in 1991

Communist state under Tito, with Croatia one of six separate republics.

1990
Multiparty elections give victory to Franjo Tuđman, a Croatian nationalist and leader of the HDZ (Croatian Democratic Union).

1991
Croatia declares independence from Yugoslavia. Croatian Serbs establish the Republic of the Serbian Krajina at Knin, driving many Croats from their

Stipe Mesić

villages with the help of the Yugoslav army. The first use of the term 'ethnic cleansing' dates from this time. War breaks out with the sieges of Dubrovnik and Vukovar.

1992
Croatia is recognized by the European Union and United Nations.

1995
Operation Storm evicts rebel Serbs from the Krajina region, leading to a mass exodus of refugees into Serbia and Bosnia. The Erdut agreement ends the war with Serbia, though parts of Slavonia, including Vukovar, remain under UN control until 1998.

1999
Death of President Tuđman.

2000
The liberal candidate Stipe Mesić is elected president.

2005
Croatia begins provisional entry talks with the European Union.

Peace & Quiet

It is not difficult to find peace and quiet in Croatia. This is a country of fewer than 5 million people, most of whom live in the major cities or on the coast. At least half of the landmass is made up of pristine wilderness in the form of mountains, forest and uninhabited islands, much of which is protected as national parks.

The coastal resorts may be heaving with bodies in summer, but it is always possible to escape to a deserted island or beach. Water-taxis ferry visitors to the more popular islands, but if you truly want seclusion, hire a motorboat or yacht instead. Be warned that the more remote the beach, the more likely it is to be officially or unofficially used by naturists. With so few people around, it hardly seems to matter and the Croatians have a very laid-back attitude to public nudity.

For real peace and quiet, head inland or go out of season. Beauty spots such as the Plitvice Lakes (▶ 21) have a completely different feel in autumn and winter, when there are few other tourists around. Unlike the Adriatic coast, inland Croatia has a continental climate and snow is common in the mountains in winter. In highland regions such as the Gorski Kotar, you need to be prepared for cold, wet weather at any time of year.

A walkway through the Plitvice Lakes National Park

National Parks

The first national park was established at the Plitvice Lakes in 1949. Croatia now has eight national parks, all in areas of great scenic beauty, where conservation is taken seriously and tourism strictly controlled. You have to pay a fee to enter these parks:-

- Nacionalni Park Brijuni (➤ 57)
- Kornati Islands (➤ 83)
- Nacionalni Park Krka (➤ 83)
- Nacionalni Park Mljet (➤ 20)
- North Velebit: mountainous region overlooking Kvarner bay
- Paklenica: limestone gorges in Velebit mountain range near Zadar
- Plitvička Jezera (Plitvice Lakes) (➤ 21)
- Risnjak (➤ 65)

Vransko Jezero: the waters and surrounding marshes are home to egrets, ducks, grebes and herons, among other birds

Nature Parks

These are typically situated in areas of population rather than wilderness. Access is generally free. The island of Lastovo is due to be added to the list.

- Biokovo: table mountain overlooking Makarska Riviera
- Kopački Rit (➤ 44)
- Lonjsko Polje (➤ 46)
- Medvednica (➤ 38)
- Papuk: mountain in central Slavonia
- Telašćica: northern extension of the Kornati Islands
- Učka: mountain dividing Istria from Rijeka
- Velebit: mountain range overlooking Kvarner bay
- Vransko Jezero: Croatia's biggest lake, near Zadar
- Žumberak-Samoborsko Gorje (➤ 49)

Wildlife

Brown bears, wolves, lynx and wild boar inhabit Croatia's national parks, particularly in the Gorski Kotar and Velebit mountain ranges and around the Plitvice Lakes. Also here is the pine-marten (*kuna*), which has given its name to Croatia's currency in reference to the time when the Romans traded its fur as exchange. Golden eagles and falcons can be seen in the Velebit Mountains, and there is a colony of griffon vultures on the island of Cres—which is also home to a large school of bottlenose dolphins.

Griffon vulture: there's a wild colony of these birds on Cres

Croatia's Famous

Marco Polo (1254–1324)
The island of Korčula claims to be the birthplace of the Venetian traveller and explorer Marco Polo, whose tales of life at the imperial court in China have captivated generations of readers. There is evidence that Polo was captured off Korčula in 1298 in a battle between the Genoese and Venetian fleets. A number of families with the surname Depolo continue to live on the island today.

Bronze statue of Tito at Kumrovec

Josip Broz Tito (1892–1980)

The man who became known as Tito was born in Kumrovec, the seventh child of a Croatian father and Slovenian mother. As a young man he served in the Austro-Hungarian military; captured and imprisoned by the Russians, he became inspired by the Bolshevik movement and fought with the Red Army. Returning to Yugoslavia, he joined the underground Communist party, adopting the name Tito in 1934.

During World War II, following the German invasion of Yugoslavia, he led the Partisan resistance against both the Ustaše régime of Croatia and the royalist Serbian Chetniks, eventually gaining Allied support. In 1945, he became leader of Yugoslavia, a position he held until his death. After splitting with Stalin in 1948, he established his own unique form of socialism, known as Titoism, and founded the Non-Aligned movement of countries which supported neither Soviet Communism nor Western capitalism.

In his personal life, Tito was a colourful character who married four times and enjoyed the company of glamorous film stars such as Italian actress Sophia Loren. Despite his liberal playboy reputation in the West, he was a ruthless dictator who suppressed all dissidence, especially in Croatia. Whatever his faults, Tito managed to hold the disparate nations of Yugoslavia together for 35 years and it was only after his death that the country fell apart.

Goran Ivanišević

Croatia's best-known sportsman was born in Split in 1971 and began playing tennis at the age of seven. In 1992, he carried the Croatian flag at the Olympic Games in Barcelona but his greatest moment came in 2001 when he won the Wimbledon championships after three previous defeats in the final and only after being given a last-minute wild-card to enter the tournament.

Returning to Split in triumph, he was greeted by 100,000 fans on the waterfront and responded by stripping down to his underwear. When he retires, he plans to open a tennis academy in Split.

A triumphant Goran Ivanišević at the 2001 Wimbledon Final

Top Ten

The Roman amphitheatre in Pula

1
Dubrovnik City Walls

74 A3

Access from Pile Gate

Daily 9–7 in summer, 9–3 in winter

None

1A, 1B, 2, 3, 4, 5, 6, 8, 9

Expensive

Dubrovnik (► 72)

A promenade around the city walls offers a magnificent panorama over Dubrovnik, with views across the restored rooftops and out to sea.

There can be no better introduction to Dubrovnik than to walk the 2km (1-mile) circuit of its medieval walls. High above the old town, you peer into secret gardens and cloisters that are out of sight at street level. From here you also get a sense of the damage caused during the 1991–2 siege, with gleaming new roof tiles illustrating the fact that over 70 per cent of houses took direct hits.

There was a wall around Dubrovnik in the 8th century, but the present walls date from the 15th-century heyday of the Ragusan republic. Up to 25m (82ft) in height and 6m (20ft) in width, they are reinforced with bastions and towers. Each of the sea-facing bastions, as well as the five gates, is protected by an effigy of Dubrovnik's patron saint, St Blaise.

Access to the ramparts is at three different places, though most people begin a circuit just inside Pile Gate (the others are at Ploče Gate and St John's Fort). Walking clockwise, you first climb to the Minčeta Tower, designed by the Florentine Michelozzo Michelozzi in 1455 and completed by Juraj Dalmatinac (George the Dalmatian), architect of Šibenik Cathedral. This is literally and metaphorically the high point of the walk, and you can climb to the roof for the best views. Continue in the same direction to pass above the Old Port and return on the seaward side.

The ticket, funds from which are used to support restoration projects, also gives access to Fort Lovrijenac, a free-standing fortress outside Pile Gate.

Pile Gate (opposite) is the main entrance to the town (inset opposite and below), fortified by its colossal encircling walls

2
Gornji Grad, Zagreb

34 C5

Cafés (£) and restaurants (££)

Tram 1, 6, 11, 12, 13, 14, 17 to Trg Bana Jelačića then funicular to Gradec

Fondacija Ivan Meštrović (► 33), Hrvatski Muzej Naivne Umjetnosti (► 36), Katedrala (► 37), Kula Lotrščak (► 37), Muzej Grada Zagreba (► 38), Trg Bana Jelačića (► 40)

Built on a wooded hillside in the 11th century, the medieval core of Gradec is now an atmospheric district of churches, palaces and cobbled streets.

The oldest part of Zagreb is situated on a hill overlooking the modern city. Although it is possible to walk up, the most enjoyable way of getting there is on the funicular railway, which departs every 10 minutes from Tomićeva, near Trg Bana Jelačića. This was the first public transport in Zagreb when it opened in 1893 and it has become a city institution. The ascent takes less than a minute and is sometimes claimed to be the shortest public transport journey in the world.

Walking ahead past the Lotrščak Tower, you soon reach Markov trg (St Mark's Square), the focal point of the Gornji Grad (Upper Town). The square has an important role as the heart of government in Croatia. On the right is the Sabor (Parliament), where independence was declared in 1991, and on the left is the Banski Dvor, the president's official residence, which was hit by a rocket attack the same year. At the heart of the square is St Mark's Church, whose colourful mosaic roof tiles feature the coats of arms of Croatia, Dalmatia, Slavonia and Zagreb.

You can get a sense of the importance of Catholicism in Croatia at the nearby Kamenita Vrata (Stone Gate), one of the original entrances to the city. When a fire in 1731 destroyed most of the surrounding houses, an image of the Virgin was found unharmed in the rubble. The gate now houses a shrine, where pilgrims can usually be found lighting candles and offering prayers to the Virgin.

KNJIŽNICA GORNJI GRAD

Lotrščak Tower, from which a cannon is fired daily at midday

3
Hvar

The sunniest island in the Adriatic is an idyllic place of lavender fields and vineyards, whose capital is fast becoming Croatia's glitziest resort.

🚩 81 D2

🚢 Ferry from Split to Stari Grad or Drvenik to Sućuraj; catamarans from Split to Hvar town and Jelsa in summer

ℹ️ Trg Svetog Stjepana, Hvar town

☎️ 021 741059

▶ Brač (▶ 82)

❓ Performances of drama and music in summer at Hvar Theatre and in the cloisters of the Franciscan Monastery

The town's marina

So confident are Hvar's hoteliers in the island's legendary climate that they offer free accommodation in the event of snow—something that happened in January 2005 for the first time in 10 years. In a typical year, the island receives over 2,700 hours of sunshine. The scent of sage and rosemary hangs in the air, and during the lavender harvest in early summer the countryside is a riot of purple colour.

The island capital, Hvar town, has been christened the 'new St Tropez' because of the number of celebrities cruising by on their private yachts. Over the last few years Hvar has become the place to be seen on the Adriatic coast and there are now numerous upmarket restaurants and chic boutiques.

The best way to arrive is undoubtedly by boat, sailing into the harbour with its waterfront houses overlooked by a Venetian fortress and medieval walls. The main square fronts directly onto the sea, with a cathedral at one end and the former Venetian arsenal at the other. The top floor of the arsenal houses one of Europe's oldest public theatres, which opened in 1612 and has recently been restored with two tiers of boxes.

Water-taxis from Hvar town take bathers to the offshore Pakleni Islands, with their rocky beaches and pinewoods. There are more good beaches at Stari Grad, the island's chief ferry port, and at Jelsa, an attractive holiday resort with views across to the mainland and boats departing in summer for the beaches of Zlatni Rat (▶ 26).

St Stephen's Cathedral in the main square

4
Mljet

🔲 81 E1

🍴 Restaurants (££) in
Polače and Pomena;
also by the lakeshore
and on St Mary's Island
in summer

🚢 Ferry or catamaran from
Dubrovnik

ℹ️ Polače

☎ 020 744086

Nacionalni Park Mljet

✉️ Prištaniste 2 (by the
lake)

☎ 020 744058

✋ Expensive

*Pine and oak trees
predominate on the
forested island of Mljet*

*This southern Adriatic island is a place of almost
mythical beauty, with pinewoods, sandy beaches
and lakes at the heart of a national park.*

According to legend, Mljet was the home of the beautiful
nymph Calypso, who in Homer's *Odyssey* seduced
Ulysses and held him prisoner for seven years in her cave
on the south coast of the island. Whatever the truth of the
story, Mljet is an island which continues to captivate
visitors today.

Most people visit Mljet on day-trips, though the island
certainly rewards a longer stay and if you spend the night
here you will virtually have it to yourself. For a brief visit,
the easiest options are the daily catamaran from Dubrovnik
or an organized excursion from resorts such as Cavtat,
Korčula and Orebić. The cost of an excursion usually
includes an entry ticket for the national park.

The boats dock at Polače, a pretty little harbourside
village built around the ruins of a Roman villa. From here, a
free national park shuttle bus takes you to Veliko Jezero,
the larger of two saltwater lakes inside the park. The ticket
also includes a boat transfer to St Mary's Island, where an
abandoned 12th-century Benedictine monastery stands
alone in the middle of the lake. Another option is to follow
the path around the lakeshore to Stari Most (Old Bridge) at
the confluence of the two lakes. If you want to explore
further, you can hire bikes here in summer; it takes about
30 minutes to cycle around Veliko Jezero, passing the
monastery on your way to the open sea.

At the other end of the island, Saplunara has one of
Croatia's finest sandy beaches.

5
Nacionalni Park Plitvička Jezera (Plitvice Lakes)

The crystalline lakes and waterfalls of the Plitvice Lakes National Park form Croatia's most spectacular natural sight, attracting over half a million visitors a year.

Even by the standards of Croatia, the Plitvice Lakes are stunning and it is well worth making the effort to get there despite the long journey from the coastal resorts. Most people come in summer, but the lakes have a different appeal throughout the seasons, covered with snow in winter and full of rushing water when the snows melt in springtime.

This was the first national park in Croatia, created in 1949. Bears, wolves and lynx roam in the fir and beech forests, though you are unlikely to see any of them. It would be easy to spend days wandering around the park on the extensive network of footpaths, and it is possible to do this by staying in one of the on-site hotels. Most visitors, however, make do with a single day, enough to get a feel for the landscape and see the most spectacular sights.

The entrance ticket includes shuttle buses and boat trips, so you can see quite a lot in a few hours. From the main entry point, Ulaz 1, a short path leads to an observation platform with views over Veliki Slap, the largest waterfall, tumbling 70m (229ft) over a cliff. From here you can walk right around and beneath the falls on specially constructed wooden bridges before taking a boat trip across Jezero Kozjak, the largest lake. If you want to explore further, information boards at the entry points suggest various colour-coded itineraries ranging from two to six hours, using a combination of walking, buses and boats.

 80 B5

 75km (47 miles) south of Karlovac, signposted from the A1 motorway

 053 751015

 Daily 8–8 in summer, 9–5 in winter

 Cafés (£) and restaurants (££) at park entrances

 Bus from Zagreb and Split

 Very expensive

Trout in one of the turquoise-coloured lakes

6
Pula Arena

56 A1

Ulica Flavijevska, Pula

052 219028

Daily 9–9, May–Sep; 9–3, Oct–Apr

None

Bus to Pula

Moderate

➤ Brijuni Islands (➤ 63), Pula (➤ 22)

? Concerts and performances in summer

The arena— still being used for entertainment (albeit of a different kind) some 2,000 years after it was built

One of the largest Roman amphitheatres ever built has been providing entertainment for the people of Pula for more than two thousand years.

Pula has grown into one of Croatia's biggest cities, but at its heart are the remains of a Roman town founded in the 1st century BC. This was an important administrative centre of around 50,000 people, with temples, town walls and a harbour. The most impressive sight by far is the huge, ruined Roman arena, the sixth largest of its kind in the world.

The arena had space for more than 20,000 spectators, who would come here to watch gladiator fights. Constructed out of local Istrian stone, the theatre was built on a slope, with the result that the outer wall has three storeys on its seaward side and two on the landward side. The lower storeys are decorated with arches while the upper level features rectangular openings. The audience sat in a semi-circle in rows of tiered seats, built to take advantage of the natural incline of the hill. In Roman times, the floor of the arena would have been covered in sand and a large awning was stretched across the roof to shield spectators from the sun.

Today the amphitheatre is still used to host concerts by the likes of Luciano Pavarotti, Placido Domingo, Joe Cocker, Jamiroquai and Sting. It is also used as a venue during the annual Pula film festival. During the day, visitors can wander freely around the arena, admiring the scale of it all. The underground passages, which once acted as prisons and cages for wild animals, now house a mildly diverting display of Roman wine jars and olive presses.

7
Rovinj

With Venetian-style houses leaning into the water, fishing boats on the quayside and wooded islands offshore, Rovinj is the gem of the Istrian coast.

🕂 56 A2

🚌 Bus from Poreč, Pula and Vrsar

ℹ️ Obala Pina Budicina 12

☎ 052 811566

➤ Vrsar and Limski Kanal (► 67)

❓ Open-air art festival on Grisia, second Sun in Aug; feast of St Euphemia, 16 Sep

A busy harbour and cobbled streets contribute to Rovinj's charm

Rovinj (Rovigno) is the perfect Croatian town. Densely packed townhouses are crowded onto a narrow peninsula, their brightly coloured façades reflected in the sea. Artists sell their work on cobbled streets. On summer evenings, tourists stroll around the harbourside, enjoying the wine bars, restaurants and ice-cream parlours,. Yet although Rovinj is undeniably popular with visitors it manages to have a life of its own.

Rovinj was built on an island which was linked to the mainland in 1763. From the large open square in front of the harbour, the Balbi Arch leads straight into the oldest part of town. The arch, built in 1680 and crowned by a Venetian winged lion, features a relief of a Turk's head on the outside and a Venetian inside, a clear message to the Turks to keep out.

A maze of steep, narrow lanes leads up to the church of St Euphemia. Most people walk up Grisia, the main street of the old town. This is always lively, especially in summer when numerous artists set up here, but the lanes to either side are more atmospheric, with unexpected hidden courtyards and alleys. The church is dedicated to a 3rd-century martyr from Asia Minor whose body washed up in Rovinj five centuries after her death. There are fabulous sunset views from the terrace.

In summer you can take a boat trip from the harbour to Crveni Otok (Red Island) to swim from its rock and pebble beaches and enjoy views of Rovinj from the water.

8

Split–Dioklecijanove Palače (Diocletian's Palace)

The ruins of a Roman palace in the heart of a modern city provide a fascinating blend of old and new.

✚ 80 C2

ℹ Peristil

☎ 021 345606

➤ Split (➤ 86)

Podrum

🕐 Mon–Sat 9–6

✋ Cheap

The central courtyard (peristyle) of the palace

Diocletian (245–c312) was born in Salona (➤ 84), the son of slaves, but rose to become emperor of Rome. Under his reign Christians were persecuted and many were put to death. It was Diocletian who laid the foundations for the division of the Roman Empire into eastern and western spheres, which later became Catholic and Orthodox—a division which continues to affect Balkan politics today.

Around AD 305 Diocletian returned to his native Dalmatia, where he lived out his years in retirement. The palace built for this purpose on the waterfront in Split became the nucleus of the modern city. Not much remains of the original palace, but as you wander around you will stumble across ancient Roman stones and columns incorporated into the houses built within the palace walls.

The best approach is through the Bronze Gate on the harbourfront Riva, which leads straight into the Podrum or underground halls. This is the best surviving part of the palace and it gives a good idea of the layout, as the rooms here stood directly beneath the main imperial apartments. A marble and mosaic dining table, believed to have been used by Diocletian, was discovered here in 1998.

The colonnaded central courtyard was known as the peristyle and it continues as a focal point today. To one side is the emperor's mausoleum, now the cathedral (➤ 87); across the square, a narrow lane leads to the Temple of Jupiter, now the baptistry, with a carved 11th-century font at its centre.

9
Varaždin

This enjoyable town to the north of Zagreb is a relaxing and prosperous place of artists, musicians and the finest baroque architecture in Croatia.

Varaždin was the capital of Croatia from 1756 to 1776 before being destroyed in a fire, started by an unfortunate young man who tripped over a pig while smoking, setting light to a haystack, and was whipped in front of the town hall for his crime. Rebuilt at the end of the 18th century, the result is a beautifully harmonious town of baroque mansions, townhouses and churches, whose traffic-free streets and squares make for some delightful strolling.

Varaždin is proud of its heritage and at times it can feel almost like a theme town, when costumed entertainers take to the streets, the city scribe sells calligraphic passports to tourists and the Changing of the Guard takes place outside the town hall, with guardsmen in bearskin hats and military uniforms performing the ceremony to the sound of drums. There are a number of historical events throughout the year, including the Varaždin Baroque Evenings in autumn, when classical concerts are held in the churches and theatres.

The greatest pleasure in Varaždin is simply wandering around the baroque centre, perhaps pausing for a coffee or an ice-cream beneath the clock tower in Trg Kralja Tomislava, the main square.

A short walk from here, the mostly 16th-century castle, Stari Grad, can be reached by crossing a drawbridge and moat. The castle, set around a beautiful three-tiered courtyard, is home to the town museum, featuring historical displays and a series of themed galleries depicting the changing tastes in furniture from the 16th to 20th centuries.

✚ 42 B3

🚌 Bus from Zagreb

🚆 Train from Zagreb

ℹ️ Ulica Ivana Padovca 3

☎ 042 210987

▶ Čakovec (► 42), Trakošćan (► 50), Zagorje (► 51)

❓ Changing of the Guard, Sat 11am, May–Oct

Stari Grad

🕐 Tue–Sun 10–6

✋ Moderate

Left: baroque detail in the cathedral
Below: the bell-tower of St John the Baptist in Tomislav Square

10
Zlatni Rat, Brač

✠ 80 C2

🍴 Bar (£) at Zlatni Rat, restaurants (££) in Bol and Murvica

🚢 Ferry from Split to Supetar; excursion boats from Jelsa to Zlatni Rat in summer

ℹ️ Polat Bolskih Pomoraca, Bol

☎ 021 635638

➤ Brač (➤ 82), Hvar (➤ 19)

The perfect beach—with shade as required

The beach that launched a thousand travel posters—a beautiful sand and shingle spit backed by pinewoods and shifting with the tides.

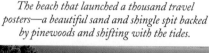

Despite having more than 5,000km (3,100 miles) of coastline, Croatia is not known for its beaches and many visitors are disappointed to find that most beaches are made up of pebbles or rocks rather than sand. One beach, however, appears on every tourist poster as an iconic image of the Adriatic coast and that is Zlatni Rat (Golden Cape, or Horn).

In truth, even this beach is not ideal for sunbathing as it is mostly composed of gravel, but the setting is magnificent. The best way to appreciate it is probably to arrive by boat, or to look down on Zlatni Rat from the summit of Vidova Gora. Set on a triangular sandbar which juts 300m (327 yards) into the sea, the beach subtly changes shape with the actions of the wind and tides. The water is shallow and shelves gently into the sea, making it safe for children, and when things get too hot there is plenty of shade to be found in the pinewoods at the centre.

Unless you have your own boat, you get there by following the 2km (1.6-mile) coastal promenade from Bol. Zlatni Rat is an incredibly popular spot in summer, with day-trippers arriving from Split and Hvar. If you want to escape the crowds, there are several pebble beaches in the rocky coves to the west, some of which are used by naturists. A cliff-top path from here leads to the village of Murvica, where you can dine at a rustic terrace *konoba* high above the sea with views across the water to Hvar.

What To See

Above: Rovinj harbour
Right: Woman in Agony *in the Meštrović Studio in Zagreb*

CROATIA

0 — 50 km
0 — 40 miles

(A)

5

(1)

4

3

2

1

Drava

■ **MARIBOR**

Čakovec

Varaždin ■ Ludbr

Trakošćan   Varaždinske
Toplice
Ivanec

Celje   Krapina

Velik Tabor   Marija
Bistrica
Kumrovec

Kranj

Sava

LJUBLJANA ■   (SLO)

A23

■ **UDINE**

Gorizia

Zaprešić   **Sesvete**

Novo Mesto ■   Samobor
Park
Prirode   **ZAGREB** ■ Velika
Žumberak-Samoborsko Gorje   Gorica

Ivani
Grac

Monfalcone   Postojna

■ **SISAK**

KARLOVAC ■   Petrinja

TRIESTE ■

Piran ■   Koper

Nacionalni Park
Risnjak   Duga
Resa

Glina

Umag ■   Buje   Buzet

RIJEKA ■   Delnice   Knrjak

Novigrad   Pazin   Opatija   Ogulin   Velika
Kladuša

Poreč   Omišalj ■   Crikvenica   Slunj

Rovinj   Žminj

Dvo

Park Šume
Zlatni Rt   Labin   Krk   Senj ■ Brinje

Vodnjan   Cres   Krk   Baška   Otočac
Nacionalni Park
Brijuni

Nacionalni Park
Plitvička
Jezera

Bihać

PULA   Cres

Rab   Pečane

Osor   Rab   Jablanac   Udbina

Mali Lošinj   Gospić   Brotnja

Lošinj   Pag   A1   Sučevići

Pag   Nacionalni Park
Paklenica

Nin   Obrovac   Knir

ZADAR ■   Benkovac   Kistanje

Ugljan   Nacionalni
Park
Krka   Drni

Dugi Otok   Pašman   Biograd

Skradin

Nacionalni Park
Kornati   **Šibenik**

Pésaro ■   Primošten

Fano

■ **ANCONA**

Macerata ■

(1)

Áscoli
Piceno

(A)   (B)   (C)

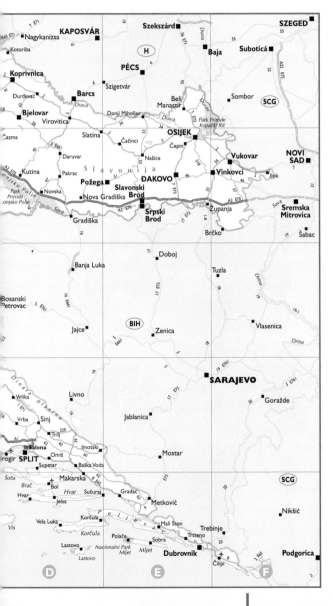

Zagreb and Inland Croatia

The vast inland region known as continental Croatia has a very different feel to the fashionable Adriatic coast. Life is harsh here — tourism has made little impact and the effects of the recent war are still clearly visible, particularly  along the historic Military Frontier that forms the border with Bosnia and Serbia. This is a region of contrasting landscapes, from the rolling hills of Zagorje to the fertile farmland of Slavonia and the flood plains of the Danube, Drava and Sava rivers, as well as Croatia's most remarkable natural sight, the waterfalls at the Plitvice Lakes. At the heart of it all is Zagreb, the lively modern capital, whose splendid Hapsburg-era architecture is an illustration of the historic links between Croatia and central Europe.

'In the morning, the bustle of the fair and the picturesque costumes of the peasantry, and in the evening, during the korzo, a goodly number of Zagreb beauties are to be seen '

ADOLF HUDOVSKI
Zagreb—A Guide for Natives and Foreigners (1892)

Stone lion in Gornji Grad

Zagreb

Zagreb can be neatly divided into two parts, known as Gornji Grad (Upper Town) and Donji Grad (Lower Town). Gornji Grad is the site of the original city, founded as a hilltop fortress in the 11th century and still an enchanting district of medieval houses and cobbled streets. Modern Zagreb is centred around Donji Grad, laid out in a grid plan during the 19th century as the city expanded to meet the needs of its growing population. Between the two stands Trg Bana Jelačića, Zagreb's central square.

What to See in Zagreb

Below: peace in the Botanical Garden

🞧 35 D3
✉ Trg Nikole Šubića Zrinskog 19
☎ 01 487 3101
🕐 Tue–Fri 10–5, Sat–Sun 10–1
🍴 Lapidarium courtyard café (£)
🚋 Tram 6, 13
🞧 Moderate
➤ Trg Bana Jelačića (➤ 40), Strossmayerova Galerija Starih Majstora (➤ 40)

ARHEOLOŠKI MUZEJ (ARCHAEOLOGICAL MUSEUM)   ✪✪

This well laid-out museum, with captions in Croatian and English, contains archaeological finds from prehistoric to Roman times. The displays start on the third floor, where you will find the star attraction, the Vučedol dove. This ceramic pot in the shape of a bird, decorated with grooved geometric designs, was excavated near Vukovar and dates back more than 4,000 years. A nearby cabinet contains the complete grave goods of a married couple from the same time, including incense burners, bowls and cups. From the Bronze Age come hoards of gold jewellery and the Idol of Dalj, a carved and engraved female figure from the 14th

DID YOU KNOW?

The Upper Town is small enough to explore on foot, but to reach some of the outlying sights you may need to use a tram. The tourist office in Trg Bana Jelačića sells the Zagreb Card, which includes unlimited public transport for three days as well as half-price entry at museums.

century BC. The museum also contains the Zagreb Mummy, brought back from Egypt in 1848 and later discovered to be wrapped in a linen shroud containing the world's longest surviving example of the Etruscan text.

FONDACIJA MEŠTROVIĆ (MEŠTROVIĆ STUDIO) ✪✪
The former home and studio of the Croatian sculptor Ivan Meštrović (1883–1962) now contains an excellent museum of his work, with more than 100 sculptures in wood, bronze and stone displayed in the courtyard, garden and house alongside the artist's original furniture. Common subjects include religious imagery and female nudes, as well as some intimate studies of his own family.

🔲 34 C4
✉ Ulica Mletačka 8
☎ 01 485 1123
🕐 Tue–Fri 10–6, Sat–Sun 10–2
♿ Moderate
► Gornji Grad (► 18), Muzej Grada Zagreba (► 38)

BOTANIČKI VRT (BOTANICAL GARDEN) ✪
With waterlily-covered lakes, an arboretum and glasshouses containing native species of plants, this landscaped garden, laid out in 1889, provides an oasis of calm a short distance away from the busy roads and railway lines of Donji Grad. It forms the centrepiece of the 'Green Horseshoe', a U-shaped promenade of parks and squares designed in the 19th century to ease the pressure on the growing city.

🔲 34 C1
✉ Trg Marka Marulića
☎ 01 484 4002
🕐 Mon–Tue 9–2.30, Wed–Sun 9–7(6 Apr–May and Sep–Oct). Closed Nov–Mar
🚋 Tram 2, 4, 9
♿ Free

ETNOGRAFSKI MUZEJ (ETHNOGRAPHIC MUSEUM) ✪
The parks of Donji Grad are surrounded by grand Austro-Hungarian buildings in the Vienna Secession, or art nouveau styles, many of them built after the earthquake of 1880 to house the great museums and cultural institutions of the city. This one, designed as a congress hall, now features displays of folk costume, jewellery and musical instruments from the various regions of Croatia. Just across the square is the Hrvatsko Narodno Kazalište (Croatian National Theatre), a typically ostentatious opera house dating from 1895.

🔲 34 B2
✉ Mažuranićev trg 14
☎ 01 482 6220
🕐 Tue–Thu 10–6, Fri–Sun 10–1
🚋 Tram 12, 13, 14, 17
♿ Moderate
► Muzej Mimara (► 39)

Croatian costumes in the Ethnographic Museum

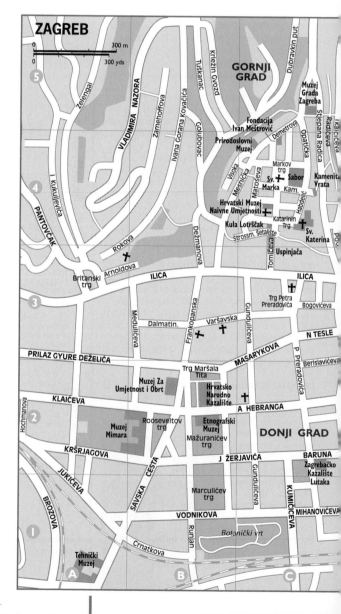

ZAGREB

0 — 300 m
0 — 300 yds

GORNJI GRAD

Muzej Grada Zagreba

Dubravkin put

Krežin Gvozd

Tuškanac

Colubovac

Ivana Gorana Kovačića

Zamenhoffova

VLADIMIRA NAZORA

Zelengaj

I Kukuljevića

PANTOVČAK

Fondacija
Ivan Meštrović

Prirodoslovni Muzej

Demetrova

Opatička

Stepana Radića

Radićeva

Visoka

Mesnička

Matoševa

Markov trg

Sv. Marka

Sabor

Marka Kam.

Kamenita Vrata

Hrvatski Muzej
Naivne Umjetnosti

Habdelić

Kula Lotrščak

Katarinin Trg

Sv. Katerina

Rokova

Arnoldova

Dežmanova

Strossm. Šetalište

Tomićeva

Uspinjača

Britanski trg

ILICA

ILICA

Trg Petra Preradovića

Bogovićeva

Medulićeva

Frankopanska

Varšavska

Gundulićeva

Dalmatin.

N TESLE

PRILAZ GYURE DEŽELIĆA

MASARYKOVA

P Preradovića

Berislavićeva

Hochmanova

Trg Maršala Tita

Muzej Za
Umjetnost i Obrt

Hrvatsko
Narodno
Kazalište

KLAIĆEVA

A HEBRANGA

Muzej Mimara

Rooseveltov trg

Etnografski Muzej

Mažuranićev trg

DONJI GRAD

KRŠRJAGOVA

J ŽERJAVIĆA

BARUNA

JUKIĆEVA

SAVSKA CESTA

Marculićev trg

Gundulićeva

Zagrebačko
Kazalište
Lutaka

KUMIČEVA

MIHANOVIĆEVA

BROZOVA

VODNIKOVA

Runjan

Botanički vrt

Crnatkova

Tehnički Muzej

A

B

C

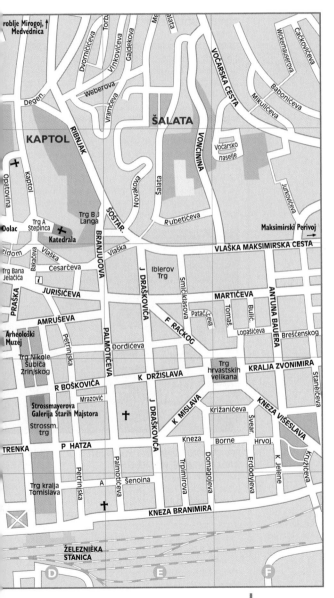

roblje Mirogoj, ↑
Medvednica

Dyorničeva
Torba
Vinkovićeva
Galdekova
Me...lata
...lata

VOČARSKA CESTA
Wickenhauserova
Cačkovićeva

Weberova
Vramčeva
Babonićeva
Mikulićeva

Degen

RIBNJAK

KAPTOL

ŠALATA

VONCININA

Vočarsko
naselje

Opatovina
Kaptol

Novakova
Šalata

Jurkovićeva

SOSTAR

Trg B J
Langa

Dolac
Trg A
Stepinca

BRANJUGOVA

Rubetićeva

Maksimirski Perivoj
→

Katedrala

zidom
Vlaška
Vlaška

VLAŠKA MAKSIMIRSKA CESTA

Bakačeva
Cesarčeva

Iblerov
Trg

Trg Bana
Jelačića
ⓘ

J DRAŠKOVIĆA
Smičiklasova
ANTUNA BAUERA

JURIŠIĆEVA

MARTIĆEVA

PRAŠKA

AMRUŠEVA

F RAČKOG
Patačićeva
Tomaš.

Bulić.
Lopašićeva
Brešćenskog

Arheološki
Muzej

Petrinjska

PALMOTIĆEVA

Đorđićeva

Trg
hrvastskih
velikana

KRALJA ZVONIMIRA

Trg Nikole
Šubića
Zrinjskog

R BOŠKOVIĆA

K DRŽISLAVA

KNEZA VIŠESLAVA

Staneljeva

Mrazović

Strossmayerova
Galerija Starih Majstora

J DRAŠKOVIĆA
K MISLAVA
Križanićeva

Kružićeva

Strossm.
trg

✝
Švear.
Hrvoj.

TRENKA

P HATZA

Kneza
Borne

K Jelene
Erdödyjeva

Petrinjska
Palmotićeva

Trg kralja
Tomislava

A
Šenoina

Trplimirova
Domagojeva

✝

KNEZA BRANIMIRA

⊠

ŽELEZNIČKA
STANICA

D   E   F

35

GORNJI GRAD (▶ 18, TOP TEN)

GROBLJE MIROGOJ (MIROGOJ CEMETERY)   ✪✪

Not many cemeteries are listed as tourist attractions, but this peaceful graveyard on the outskirts of Zagreb is undoubtedly a special place. It was designed by Hermann Bollé (1845–1926), who also worked on the cathedral, as a resting-place for the citizens of Zagreb. Behind a high wall topped by green cupolas, Catholic, Orthodox, Muslim and Jewish tombstones are found side by side, along with others adorned with the five-pointed Communist star. The arcades to either side of the main entrance contain some impressive monuments to members of Croatia's noble families. Among those buried here is Franjo Tuđman (1922–99), the first president of independent Croatia, whose black granite tomb attracts numerous visitors to light candles and lay flowers at his grave.

Left: the Mirogoj Cemetery

Right: Ivan Generalić's self-portait in the Naïve Art Museum (www.generalic.com)

HRVATSKI MUZEJ NAIVNE UMJETNOSTI   ✪✪
(CROATIAN NAÏVE ART MUSEUM)

The Croatian naïve art movement originated in the 1930s in the village of Hlebine (▶ 43) and soon developed an international reputation. Most of the artists were self-taught peasant painters, who used simple techniques and primary colours to portray scenes of rural life. This small museum contains a good overview of the movement, including its two key figures Ivan Generalić (1914–92) and his son Josip Generalić (1936–2004). Petar Smajić's (1910–85) wooden sculptures of *Adam and Eve* and *Mother and Child* are full of expression.

KATEDRALA (CATHEDRAL) ✪✪

The twin neo-Gothic spires of Zagreb's cathedral tower over the city, dominating the views as you approach. It is dedicated to St Stephen and St Ladislaus. There was a church here as early as 1102, but the present neo-Gothic cathedral was built 800 years later by the architect Hermann Bollé following an earthquake which destroyed much of Zagreb in 1880. Behind the altar is the sarcophagus of Cardinal Alojzije Stepinac (1898–1960), a former archbishop of Zagreb who was placed under house arrest by the Tito régime; he was beatified by the Pope John Paul during a visit to Croatia in 1988, the first step on the road to sainthood. His actual tomb, in the north wall, features a relief by Ivan Meštrović depicting the bishop kneeling humbly before Christ. The nearby sacristy contains some 13th-century frescoes from an earlier cathedral on this site.

➕ 35 D4
✉ Kaptol 31
☎ 01 481 4727
🕐 Daily 8–8
🚃 Tram 1, 6, 11, 12, 13, 14, 17 to Trg Bana Jelačića
💵 Free
▶ Trg Bana Jelačića (▶ 40)

Left: one of Ivan Generalić's works in the Naïve Art Museum (www.generalic.com)

Right: the cathedral spires in Zagreb

KULA LOTRŠČAK (BURGLARS' TOWER) ✪✪

The firing of the Grič cannon from the Burglars' Tower at midday has become an essential feature of Zagreb life and it is worth timing your visit to coincide with the ritual. The tower, which takes its name from the 'bell of thieves' that once chimed each night as a warning at the closing of the city gates, is the only remaining part of the 13th-century fortifications. It is said that the citizens of Zagreb set their watches when they hear the blast. Climb the spiral staircase just before noon to watch the ceremony, performed by a cannoneer in blue uniform, then continue to the observation platform for the best city views.

➕ 34 C4
✉ Strossmayerovo Šetalište 9
☎ 01 485 1768
🕐 Tue–Sun 11–8, May–Oct,
🚠 Funicular to Gradec
💵 Inexpensive
▶ Gornji Grad (▶ 18), Hrvatski Muzej Naivne Umjetnosti (▶ 36)

🔲 35 off F4
✉ Maksimirska Cesta
🚋 Tram 11,12

Zoo
☎ 01 230 2199
🕐 Daily 9–8 in summer, 9–5
in winter (ticket office
closed one hour before
closing times)
💵 Moderate

🔲 42 B2
🚋 Tram 15 then cable-car
💵 Cable-car: Moderate

---

*Right: exhibit in Zagreb's
City Museum*

🔲 34 C5
✉ Ulica Opatička 20
☎ 01 485 1364
🕐 Tue–Fri 10–6, Sat–Sun
10–1
🍴 Stara Vura restaurant (££)
and café (£)
💵 Moderate
➤ Gornji Grad (► 18),
Fondacije Meštrović
(► 33)

MAKSIMIRSKI PERIVOJ (MAKSIMIR PARK) ✪✪

When the people of Zagreb want to relax, they hop on a tram to Maksimir Park. At weekends the park is crowded out with local families who come here to walk, cycle and enjoy the fresh air. Opened in 1794, this was one of the first public parks in Europe, and with its belvederes, follies, bridges and lakeside paths it retains an enjoyably old-fashioned feel. Children will enjoy the zoo, with its surprisingly large collection of animals including lions, tigers, elephants and bears. Just across from the park is the Maksimir stadium, home of the Croatian national football team and the local favourites Dinamo Zagreb.

MEDVEDNICA ✪✪

The mountain range of Medvednica overlooks Zagreb to the north, offering numerous hiking trails and woodland paths within easy reach of the city. It is quite an effort to get there but the journey is all part of the fun. Take tram 8 or 14 to the Mihaljevac terminus, then transfer to tram 15 for the short hop to Dolje. From here, walk through a tunnel and climb a short path to reach the lower station for the *žičara* (cable-car). The cars leave on the hour for the 20-minute ascent to the summit of Sljeme (1,035m/3,384ft), with dramatic views all the way. There are restaurants near the summit, shady picnic meadows and in winter there are even ski slopes here. A short walk leads to the Church of Our Lady of Sljeme, built in 1932 to celebrate 1,000 years of Christianity in Croatia. If you are feeling energetic, you can take the cable-car to the summit and walk back down through the beech woods.

MUZEJ GRADA ZAGREBA ✪✪✪
(MUSEUM OF THE CITY OF ZAGREB)

This enjoyable museum manages the difficult task of bringing Zagreb's complex history to life through an entertaining series of models, reconstructions, themed galleries and interactive displays. Much of the material is arranged chronologically, but there are also rooms devoted to topics such as shopping, theatres, clubs and societies, war and daily life. The tour of the museum, housed in a 17th-century convent, begins with a walk through an Iron Age metal workshop,

recently excavated beneath the site. From the founding of
Zagreb in 1094 and the 'free and royal city' of Gradec in
1242, the museum tells the story of Zagreb all the way up
to 1991, when Serbian rockets hit the nearby presidential
palace. The event is recalled with dramatic video
footage and a poignant display of broken
crockery and furniture.

Venetian glass and The
Bather *by Renoir, both in
the Mimara Museum in
Zagreb*

MUZEJ MIMARA (MIMARA MUSEUM) ✪✪

This extensive museum is based on the personal collection
of the Croatian businessman Ante Topić Mimara
(1898–1987), who spent his life amassing an eclectic range
of artworks from around the world and donated them to
the nation before his death. The extraordinary collection
includes ancient Egyptian glassware, Chinese and
Japanese porcelain, Persian carpets, Russian and
Byzantine icons, a carved ivory English hunting-horn, Italian
Renaissance painting and sculpture, and works by Rubens,
Rembrandt and Renoir.

✚ 34 A2
✉ Rooseveltov Trg 4
☎ 01 482 8100
🕐 Tue–Wed and Fri–Sat
   10–5, Thu 10–7, Sun
   10–2
🍴 Café (£)
🚊 Tram 12, 13, 14, 17
✋ Moderate
➤ Etnografski Muzej (➤ 33)

39

📍 35 D2
✉ Trg Nikole Šubića Zrinskog 11
☎ 01 489 5117
🕐 Tue 10–1, 5–7, Wed–Sun 10–1
🚋 Tram 6, 13
💲 Inexpensive
➤ Arheološki Muzej (➤ 32)

STROSSMAYEROVA GALERIJA STARIH MAJSTORA (STROSSMAYER GALLERY OF OLD MASTERS) ⭐⭐

Bellini, Botticelli, Carpaccio, Lippi, Tintoretto—the great painters of the Italian Renaissance also worked in Croatia and this gallery clearly indicates Croatia's role in the mainstream of European art. It was founded in 1868 by Bishop Josip Juraj Strossmayer (1815–1905), a leading Croatian nationalist and supporter of Croat-Serb unity. A statue of Strossmayer by Ivan Meštrović stands outside the building. Look in the entrance lobby for the Baška stone, an 11th-century tablet from the island of Krk containing the oldest known example of the Glagolitic script. South of here, beyond the ornate cream-coloured Art Pavilion, is an equestrian statue of Tomislav, the first king of Croatia, crowned in AD 925.

DID YOU KNOW?

The tie, symbol of businessmen around the world, originated in Croatia. The silk scarves worn by Croatian officers during the Thirty Years War (1618–48) caught on in fashionable French society, where the custom of dressing with a necktie was known as à la croate—later adapted to cravate.

Dolac market—great for fruit, veg and flowers

📍 35 D3
🚋 Tram 1, 6, 11, 12, 13, 14, 17
ℹ Trg Bana Jelačića 11
☎ 01 481 4051
➤ Gornji Grad (➤ 18), Arheološki Muzej (➤ 32), Katedrala (➤ 37)

TRG BANA JELAČIĆA ⭐⭐⭐

With its clanking trams, newspaper kiosks, flower stalls and open-air cafés, this broad square is the focal point of Zagreb and the best place to take the pulse of the city. This is where people meet to start the evening *korzo*, a ritual stroll to see and be seen. At the centre of the square is an equestrian statue of Governor Josip Jelačić (1801–59), an iconic figure in Croatian nationalism; during the Tito years, the statue was removed and dismantled but it was returned here in 1990. Just above the square, on a raised terrace, is Zagreb's colourful central market, where farmers sell fresh produce on weekday mornings.

Zagreb Old Town

This short walk takes you from Trg Bana Jelačića into the heart of Gornji Grad, with the option of a funicular ride. The best time for walking is during the early evening, joining the citizens of Zagreb on their *korzo* or promenade.

Start in Trg Bana Jelačića and head west along Ilica, Zagreb's main shopping street. Take the first right into Ulica Tomića usually known as Tomićeva.

You can ascend to the upper town by funicular or by climbing the flight of steps. Either way, you arrive on the Strossmayerovo Šetalište promenade, opposite Kula Lotrščak (► 37).

Continue straight ahead beside the tower, passing a Greek Orthodox church and the Naïve Art Museum (► 36) to arrive in Markov trg (St Mark's Square), dominated by the colourful roof tiles of St Mark's Church.

This square is the heart of the Croatian government, with the presidential palace on your left and the Sabor (Parliament) on your right.

Turn right along Ulica Kamenita and walk through the Kamenita Vrata (Stone Gate), where pilgrims light candles at the shrine. Take the steps to the right beside a statue of George and the Dragon to walk down Ulica Radićva. Turn left onto Krvavi Most (Bloody Bridge) and cross the bridge to reach Ulica Tkalčiceva, a pretty street of 19th-century houses and trendy open-air bars. Continue straight ahead to reach the upper level of Dolac market, then take the steps down to your right to return to Trg Bana Jelačića.

Distance
2km (1 mile)

Time
1 hour

Start/end point
Trg Bana Jelačića
➕ 35 D3
🚊 Tram 1, 6, 11, 13, 14, 17

Lunch
Kerempuh (££)
✉ Dolac market
☎ 01 481 9000

St Mark's Church and one of Gornji Grad's steep alleyways

41

What to See in Inland Croatia

ČAKOVEC ☉

Čakovec is the main town of the Međimurje, a region of fertile farmland between the Mura and Drava rivers close to the Hungarian border. The town's history dates to 1546, when the Hapsburg emperor Ferdinand I awarded it to the Zrinski family in recognition of their services in battles against the Ottoman Turks. Their castle is now the Museum of the Međimurje, with an enjoyable collection of Carnival masks, a recreated pharmacy and works by local artists. Zrinski Park, between the castle and town centre, contains a monument to Nikola Zrinski (1620–64), a governor of Croatia who was killed by a wild boar while out hunting.

ĐAKOVO ☉

If you are driving around eastern Slavonia, Đakovo makes a good place to spend the night or to break the journey back to Zagreb. The main sight is the red-brick cathedral, whose twin spires, 84m (275ft) tall, tower over the city. This is the third cathedral on this site; it was built between 1866 and 1882 by Bishop Josip Juraj Strossmayer, a leading figure in 19th-century Croatian nationalism. A short walk along Ulica

ČAKOVEC sidebar:
🔲 Below B3
🚌 Bus from Varaždin
ℹ️ Trg Kralja Tomislava 1
☎ 040 313319
► Varaždin (► 25)

Castle
⏰ Tue–Fri 10–3, Sat–Sun 10–1
💶 Moderate

ĐAKOVO sidebar:
🔲 43 E1
ℹ️ Ulica Kralja Tomislava 3
☎ 031 812319
► Osijek (► 48), Slavonski Brod (► 48), Vukovar (► 50)

INLAND CROATIA

0 — 50 km
0 — 30 miles

Murski Središče · Čakovec · Gotičan · Kotoriba · Nagykanizsa
Gornje Vratno · Prelog · Nagyatád
Donja Voća · Drava · Ludbreg · Drnje · Hlebine
Trakošćan · Varaždin · Varaždinske Toplice · Reka · Koprivnica
Lepoglava · Novi Maruf · Kalnik · Novigrad Podravski · Đurđevac
Hum na Sutli · Desinić · Pregrada · Krapina · Rádoboj · Zlatar · Breznica · Zlatar Bistrica · Križevci · Pitomača
Celje · Veliki Tabor · Poznanovec · Sv. Ivan Zabno · Rovišće · Veliko Trojstvo · Sandrovac
Kumrovec · Zabok · Marija Bistrica · Sv. Ivan Zelina · Vrbovec · Bjelovar · Narta · Velika Pisanica
Krško · V. Trgovišće · G. Bistra · Kašina · Dubrava · Veliki Grđevac · Grubišno Polje
Zaprešić · Polatno · Sljeme · Sesvete · Dugo Selo · Kloštar Ivanić · Čazma · Samarica · Veliki Zdenci
ZAGREB · Ivanić-Grad · G. Garešnica · Hercegovac · Daruvar
Novo Mesto · Samobor · Rude · Stupnik · Velika Gorica · Topolje · Humka · Garešnica · Dežanovac
Park Prirode Žumberak-Samoborsko Gorje · Klinča Sela · Kupinečki Kraljevec · Buševec · Popovača · Kutina · Banova Jaruga · Pakrac
Krašić · Kupinec · Kravarsko · Lekenik · Budaševo · Muzilovčica · Lipovljani · Novska
Ozalj · Donja Kupčina · St. Farkašić · SISAK · Topolovac · Cigoč · Lonja · Krapje · Okučani
Grić · Šiljakovič · Mošćenica · Blinjski Kut · Sunja · Park Prirode Lonjsko Polje · Jasenovac
KARLOVAC · Petrinja · Blinja · Hrvatska Kostajnica · Hrvatska Dubica
Moravice · Duga Resa · Brezovica · Čremušnica · Prekopa · Glina · Dragotina · Kozarska Dubica
Vrbovsko · Bosiljevo · Krnjak · Gvozd · Petrovac · Krstinja · Zrinska gora · Priseka · Una
Ogulin · Bijelolasica · Oštarije · Blagaj · Velika Kladuša · Gvozdansko · Dvor · Kotarani
Jasenak · Josipdol · Vojnovac · Slunj · Plaški · Radojčići

Đakovo cathedral

Matije Gupca leads to a Lippizaner stud farm, where the famous white horses are bred and trained.

HLEBINE ●●

The village of Hlebine was the birthplace of naïve art in Croatia and it is still home to several painters and sculptors producing vivid scenes of rural life. Their work can be seen at Galerija Hlebine, which also has a room devoted to Ivan Generalić (1914–92), considered the father of the Croatian naïve art movement.

🚩 Below C3

Galerija Hlebine
✉ Trg Ivana Generalića 15
☎ 048 836075
🕐 Mon–Fri 10–4, Sat 10–2
💲 Inexpensive

43 E2
☎ 031 752320
◷ Daily 8–4
🍴 Café (£) at park entrance;
Kormoran restaurant (££)
inside the park
🚤 Boat trips three or
four times daily,
Mar–Nov (£££)
▣ Free
► Osijek (► 48)

*Boardwalks through
the wetlands in the
Kopački Rit Nature
Park mean visitors get a
good view of the plants
and other wildlife*

PARK PRIRODE KOPAČKI RIT ●●

Situated on the border with Serbia at the confluence of the
Danube and Drava rivers, the Kopački Rit wetlands form a
valuable wildlife habitat for numerous species of nesting
and migrant birds. During the 1991–5 war, the park was

occupied by Serbian
troops, but it is now
clear of landmines
and open once again
to visitors. Get there
by following signs
from Bilje, 8km (5
miles) north of
Osijek on the main
road to Hungary. On
a brief visit, start
with a boat trip on the *Orao I*,
which leaves from a jetty near
the park entrance. Herons and
cormorants are common
sights, and you may see
kingfishers and black storks.
Deeper into the park are
footpaths which lead through
poplar and oak forests, where
members of the Hapsburg
aristocracy used to hunt deer and wild boar. The visitor
centre at the park entrance is a good source of
information, maps and souvenirs.

🗺 42 B3
🚌 Bus from Zagreb
🚆 Train from Zagreb
► Zagorje (► 51)

Muzej Evolucije
✉ Šetalište V Sluge
☎ 049 371491
◷ Daily 8–6 in summer,
Tue–Fri 10–3 in winter
▣ Inexpensive

KRAPINA ●

The town at the centre of the Zagorje region (► 51) is
famous for the discovery of *Homo Krapinensis* (Krapina
Man), a Neanderthal human who lived in caves some
30,000 years ago and whose remains were excavated and
studied by Croatian archaeologist Dragutin Gorjanović
Kramberger in 1899. Around 900 human bones were
unearthed on the Hušnjakovo hill, making it one of the
richest collections of human fossils in the world, though
unfortunately a complete skeleton was never found. Most
of the originals are now kept in the Croatian Natural History
Museum in Zagreb, though the Muzej Evolucije (Museum
of Evolution) in Krapina has reproductions of skulls and
bones from various mammals, including wolves, bears,
rhino and deer. A path behind the museum leads up the
hill to the cave where the bones were discovered, now
marked by somewhat artificial sculptures of prehistoric
cavemen and animals.

KUMROVEC ✪✪

This small village close to the Slovenian border is best known as the birthplace of Tito (➤ 14). These days, people come here for two reasons—to pay homage to the former Yugoslav leader and to experience the feel of rural life at the turn of the 20th century, when Tito was growing up here. The house in which he was born stands near the entrance to the village, with a statue outside and an exhibition inside giving a slightly revisionist account of Tito's place in history.

A short walk along the main street leads to the school which Tito attended from 1900 to 1905. However, the main interest is in wandering around the Staro Selo (Old Village), where cottages, farmhouses, granaries, barns and stables have been restored as an open-air museum of rural life. Among them is the blacksmith's workshop once owned by Tito's family. In summer, there are exhibitions of craftmaking (pottery, weaving, wooden toys, wine, cider) in the various studios and an old wine-cellar serving cottage cheese parcels from Zagorje. Despite the theme-park atmosphere, Kumrovec is still a working agricultural village and you see farmers on tractors and in the fields side by side with the museum exhibits.

➕ 42 A2
🚌 Bus from Zagreb
➤ Veliki Tabor (➤ 50), Zagorje (➤ 51)

Staro Selo
☎ 049 500476
🕐 Daily 9–7, Apr–Oct; 9–4, Nov–Mar
🍴 Cafés (£) and restaurants (££)
♿ Moderate

Tito's birthplace in Kumrovec

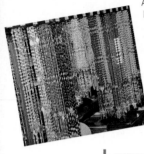

🔢 42 C1

Information centre
- ✉ Čigoć 26
- ☎ 044 715115
- 🕐 Daily 8–4

PARK PRIRODE LONJSKO POLJE ❶❶❶

The flood plains of the River Sava have been designated a nature park, preserving not only a fragile environment but also a peaceful way of life. Visitors come here in spring and summer to see the nesting white storks, one of the largest populations in Europe. Between April and August, almost every house in the village of Čigoć has a stork's nest on the roof. The people of the Lonjsko Polje live in traditional oak cottages, with external wooden staircases leading up to the first floor and chimney-less attics where hams and sausages are cured. There are good examples in all of the villages, but the greatest concentrations are in Čigoć and Krapje. Just outside Krapje is Krapje Đol, Croatia's first ornithological reserve, where herons and other waterfowl can often be seen. The information office in Čigoć can issue maps of local walks.

🔢 42 B2
- 🚌 Bus from Zagreb
- 🏢 Zagrebačka 66
- ☎ 049 468380
- ► Zagorje (► 51)

Rosaries for sale, the start of the Way of the Cross and the colourful spire of the Sanctuary of St Mary of the Snows (Marija Bistrica), a major pilgrimage centre

MARIJA BISTRICA ❶❶

Croatia's leading Marian shrine is situated north of Zagreb at the entrance to the Zagorje (► 51). Catholic pilgrims from Croatia and abroad come here to pay homage to a dark wooden statue of the Virgin to which miraculous powers have been attributed. The present church was built to house the statue in 1883 and was designed by Hermann Bollé, architect of Zagreb cathedral. On feast days, huge open-air masses are held in the amphitheatre behind the church. You can climb the Via Crucis (Way of the Cross) for the best views. Shops in the main square sell religious souvenirs as well as giant decorated gingerbread hearts, a speciality of this region.

Lonjsko Polje

This half-day circuit follows the main route through the Lonjsko Polje wetlands.

Start in Sisak, following signs towards the Autocesta (motorway) and crossing the river Sava. After 5km (3 miles), turn right on a minor road signposted to Lonja.

You pass through Budaševo, with orchards lining the road and a tall pink church spire ahead, before reaching Topolovac, a pretty village in the shadow of Sisak's industrial estate.

Keep straight ahead at a crossroads towards Lonja. The road clings to the east bank of the Sava before leaving the river to enter Čigoć. Continue on this road to Mužilovčica and Lonja.

After Lonja, the road deteriorates and there is a short section of unmade track, passing a wide bend in the river before entering a forest.

Emerging by a bridge, keep straight on towards Jasenovac on the surfaced road. The road continues on a raised dyke above the flood plain, passing through Puska on its way to Krapje, a village known for its traditional wooden architecture.

Returning to the river at Drenov Bok, you see on your left a path to the ornithological reserve at Krapje Đol.

After another 7km (4 miles), you pass under a railway bridge. Turn right immediately to cross the River Sava either by ferry or by the road bridge, destroyed during the war but under reconstruction.

The road passes through cornfields on its way to Hrvatska Dubica, a small town on the Bosnian border with much visible war damage.

Turn right just before the church to return to Sisak on the main road.

Distance
136km (84 miles)

Time
3 hours

Start/end point
Sisak

⊞ 42 B1

Lunch
Ravlić (££)

✉ Mužilovčica 72
☎ 044 710151

Horses roam free in the Lonjsko Olje Nature Park

OSIJEK ●●

+ 43 E2
ℹ Županijska 2
☎ 031 203755
► Đakovo (► 42), Kopački Rit (► 44), Vukovar (► 50)

The largest city in eastern Croatia stands on the south bank of the River Drava. The main attraction is Tvrđa, an 18th-century fortress town 2km (1 mile) east of the centre. Heavily damaged by shelling in 1991, this is now an enjoyable district of cobbled streets, churches, palaces and

defensive walls. At the centre of the main square is a plague column, erected in 1729 to give thanks for deliverance from the disease. A riverside footpath connects Tvrđa to the city centre; you can cross the suspension bridge to reach the north bank for views across the river. Osijek makes a good base for visiting the Kopački Rit Nature Park (► 44).

SAMOBOR ●●

+ 42 A2
🚌 Bus from Zagreb
ℹ Trg Kralja Tomislava 5
☎ 01 336 0044

This pleasing country town is just 20km (12 miles) from Zagreb, making it a popular day out from the capital. Pretty, pastel-coloured townhouses surround the main square,

Detail from the Plague Memorial in Tvrđa

where a stream runs beneath an onion-domed church. Viennese-style pastry shops around the square sell *samoborska kremšnita*, a rich custard tart. The whole town has an air of prosperity, helped by the number of weekend visitors from Slovenia, Austria and Zagreb. Just outside Samobor are the green hills of the Žumberak-Samoborsko Gorje (► 49).

SLAVONSKI BROD ●

+ 43 D1
🚌 Bus from Zagreb
ℹ Trg Pobjede 30
☎ 035 445765
► Đakovo (► 42)

This town on the River Sava grew up around its star-shaped fortress, built in the 18th century on the Military Frontier between the Ottoman and Hapsburg empires. During the recent war, the fortress was

repeatedly attacked from across the river by Bosnian Serbs in the town of Bosanski Brod. The town is currently undergoing extensive reconstruction. A short walk along the riverbank leads to an 18th-century Franciscan monastery with a peaceful cloister at its centre.

The cool calm of the cloisters at the monastery in Slavonski Brod

The Žumberak Hills

The Park Prirode Žumberak-Samoborsko Gorje occupies a beautiful green region of beech and chestnut forests, alpine meadows, orchards, vineyards and rural villages between Samobor and the Slovenian border.

Begin in Samobor, following signs to Jastrebarsko. On the outskirts of town, turn left to enter the Gradna river valley. After passing through the village of Rude the road climbs steeply into the woods before dropping down to a spectacular vista of the Plešivica vineyards.

This is part of the Plešivica Wine Route, where producers around the village of Plešivica advertise wine for sale.

The road descends to Jastrebarsko. Turn right towards Karlovac and stay on this road for 20km (13 miles). After crossing the Kupa–Kupa canal, just before entering Karlovac, turn right towards Ozalj, crossing a bridge over the River Kupa on your way to the town. Arriving at Ozalj, fork right towards Krašić, crossing the river once again.

Look left to see the castle at Ozalj, high on a bluff overlooking the river.

The road passes through cornfields and woods on its way to Krašić.

This small village is a popular place of pilgrimage—it was the home town of Cardinal Stepinac where he spent his final years under house arrest.

Drive through the centre of the village and turn left to Pribić. From here, the road continues for another 50km (30 miles) through the wild Žumberak hills and forests, with sweeping views across valleys and mountains into Slovenia.

Eventually you reach Bregana, where you will see a border post to your left.

Fork right here and turn right again to return to Samobor.

Distance
124km (77 miles)

Time
3 hours

Start/end point
Samobor

🔢 42 A2

Lunch
Ivančić (££)

✉ Plešivica 45
☎ 01 629 3303

Harvest time

49

42 B3
📞 042 796422
🕐 Daily 9–6 in summer, 9–3 in winter
🎫 Moderate
► Varaždin (► 25), Zagorje (► 51)

The stout defences of Trakošćan castle

DID YOU KNOW?

The first castle at Veliki Tabor was built in the 12th century for the counts of Celje. A legend tells of Veronika, a local beauty who eloped with the count's son. When the couple were captured, Veronika was killed and her body walled into the castle. During restoration work in 1982 a woman's skull was discovered in the walls.

42 A2
📞 049 434969
🕐 Daily 9–6
🎫 Inexpensive
► Kumrovec (► 45), Zagorje (► 51)

📌 43 F2
ℹ Strossmayerova 15
📞 032 442889
► Đakovo (► 42), Osijek (► 48)

TRAKOŠĆAN ⭐⭐⭐

One of the best-known sights in Croatia is this fairytale castle, standing proud on a wooded hillside, its white walls, battlements and towers reflected in an artificial lake. Although the castle dates from the 13th century, its current appearance is the result of 19th-century restoration by the owners, the Drašković family. Confiscated by the state during the Tito years, the castle is now a museum of aristocratic life, its salons filled with family portraits, firearms and antique furniture. There are walks in the parkland, and a path leads around the lake; in summer there is also a floating café with pedal-boats for hire.

VARAŽDIN (► 25, TOP TEN)

VELIKI TABOR ⭐⭐

This fine 16th-century castle stands on a hill above the village of Desinić. The displays are not as interesting as those at Trakošćan (see above) and the castle is not as well preserved, but it is worth visiting for the magnificent views across the Zagorje (► 51) from the semi-circular towers. Occasional displays of swordsmanship are held in the courtyard by actors in military costume.

VUKOVAR ⭐⭐⭐

Do not go to Vukovar and expect to enjoy it, but go anyway to reflect on the horror of war and to understand why this small town on the Danube plays such an important part in the Croatian psyche. For three months in 1991, it came under siege from Serbian forces; deprived of food and water, the inhabitants were forced out of their homes. Many escaped to safety across the cornfields but at least 2,000 people were killed and their bodies dumped in mass graves. Vukovar today is a shadow of its once prosperous self. Few of the survivors have returned and many of the houses are no more than empty shells. A bleak memorial by the riverbank pays tribute to the dead.

War-damaged buildings in
Vukovar

In the town cemetery, on the road to Ilok, rows of unmarked white crosses record the victims who were never found. Vukovar is a name which is etched on the conscience of the Balkans, and a visit here is a powerful, moving experience.

ZAGORJE ✪✪✪

With its rolling green meadows, hilltop castles and churches, vineyards, pretty villages and spa towns, the Zagorje region, north of Zagreb, is a place of legendary beauty in Croatia. The main attractions are the castles at Trakošćan (➤ 50) and Veliki Tabor (➤ 50), the pilgrimage church at Marija Bistrica (➤ 46) and the ethnographic museum at Kumrovec (➤ 45), but the real appeal of this region lies in getting off the beaten track and soaking up the atmosphere of bucolic rural life.

➕ 42 B2
➤ Krapina (➤ 44), Kumrovec (➤ 45), Marija Bistrica (➤ 46), Trakošćan (➤ 50), Varaždin (➤ 25), Veliki Tabor (➤ 50)

Pastoral scenery in the
Zagorje region

In the Know

10
Ways To Be A Local

Try to learn a few words of the Croatian language—it is always appreciated and even a simple *dobar dan* goes a long way.

Get chatting to the locals in cafés and bars, but be careful to avoid sensitive subjects such as the recent war.

Dress up and join in with the evening *korzo*, a ritual promenade when the people come out in their trendiest clothes to see and be seen.

Shop in local markets for fabulous fresh produce.

Drink strong, sweet Turkish coffee.

Tuck into huge ice-cream sundaes—whatever the weather.

Travel around on local buses and ferries—they are mostly excellent and reliable.

Go to a football match—the big teams are Dinamo Zagreb and Hajduk Split.

Strip off on the beach if you like, but cover up elsewhere, especially when visiting churches.

Relax, take your time and settle into the Mediterranean pace of life.

10
Places To Have Lunch By The Sea

Doručak Kod Tihane (££)
✉ Obala Sveti Jurja 5, Vis
☎ 021 718472
Great fish and seafood on a chic harbourside promenade.

Galija (£££)
✉ Vuličevićeva 1, Cavtat
☎ 020 478566
Top-quality Dalmatian cuisine on a terrace beneath the pine trees.

Kapetanova Kuča (£££)
✉ Mali Ston
☎ 020 754555
Fresh oysters on the Pelješac Peninsula.

Konoba Marija (££)
✉ Murvica, Brač
☎ 091 524 7439
Rustic grill in a fabulous setting high above the sea.

Lokanda Peskarija (££)
✉ Na Ponti, Dubrovnik
☎ 020 324750
Good, no-nonsense fish restaurant by the old harbour in Dubrovnik.

Morski Konjic (££)
✉ Šetalište Petra Kanavelića, Korčula
☎ 020 711878
Great views across the water to the Pelješac Peninsula.

Orhan (£££)
✉ Od Tabakarije 1, Dubrovnik
☎ 020 414183
Smart fish restaurant with a harbourside terrace outside Dubrovnik's city walls.

Tony (££)
✉ Sućuraj, Hvar
☎ No phone
Down-to-earth fishermen's bar beside the ferry port.

Veli Jože (££)
✉ Ulica Svetog Križa 3, Rovinj
☎ 052 816337
Traditional Istrian cuisine by the harbour.

Viking (£££)
✉ Limski Kanal
☎ 052 448223
Fresh fish, oysters and mussels from the Lim Fjord.

Whatever you do, take it easy

10
Top Activities

• **Canoeing and kayaking:** local tour operators offer excursions on the Cetina, Dobra and Kupa rivers
• **Cycling:** there are several bike routes in Istria
• **Diving:** there are scuba-diving schools at most resorts
• **Rafting:** in the Cetina Gorge and on the Una river
• **Rock climbing:** in the Paklenica and North Velebit national parks
• **Sailing:** you can charter yachts all along the coast
• **Swimming:** from thousands of rock and pebble beaches
• **Tennis:** most large hotels have courts
• **Walking:** in the Biokovo and Velebit mountain ranges just inland from the Dalmatian coast
• **Windsurfing:** on Brač and the Pelješac Peninsula

Rock-climbing in the Paklenica National Park and a stretch of the Dalmatian coast, where you can swim and sail

5
Good Sandy Island Beaches

• Baška, Krk
• Lopar, Rab
• Lumbarda, Korčula
• Saplunara, Mljet
• Šunj, Lopud

Buy that souvenir tie

5
Good Buys

• Croata silk tie
• Lavender from Hvar
• *Licitarsko srce* (iced gingerbread hearts) from Zagreb
• Truffles from Istria
• Wines, spirits and liqueurs

Istria and Kvarner

Although it includes some of Croatia's biggest holiday resorts, Istria feels like a different country altogether. Between the world wars, this northern Adriatic peninsula was part of Italy and it is still the most Italian place in Croatia. Many of the towns have both Italian and Croatian names and the cultural influences owe as much to Venice as to Zagreb. The hill towns of inland Istria, surrounded by vineyards and olive groves, are reminiscent of northern Italy and local farmers scour the woods for truffles each autumn. In summer, the west coast is buzzing with tourists, who crowd out the waterfront cafés, admire the work of pavement artists and soak up the Mediterranean atmosphere. Between Istria and Dalmatia is Kvarner bay, home to Croatia's two largest islands as well as its grandest Hapsburg-era resort.

> *'Istria is a long boring place wedged into the Adriatic, peopled by ignorant Slavs who wear red caps and colossal breeches'*

JAMES JOYCE (1882–1941),
letter from Pula (1904)

———————●———————

Rab town, midway along the island's west coast

Remnants of the Byzantine fortress on the largest of the Brijuni Islands, Veli Brijun

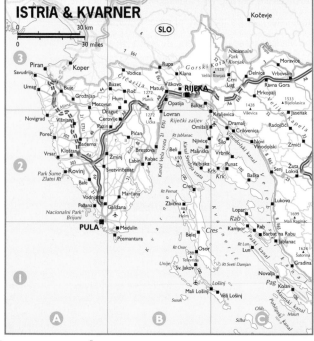

ISTRIA & KVARNER

What to See in Istria and Kvarner

NACIONALNI PARK BRIJUNI ✪✪✪

The beautiful island of Veli Brijun was used by the Yugoslav leader Tito as his summer retreat. For six months of every year, he would stay here in his villa, entertaining world leaders and running the country while hunting in his private game reserve. The island is still used by government officials but these days it is also at the centre of a national park. The easiest way to get there is on a boat trip from the fishing port of Fažana. This gives you several hours on the island, and the ticket includes a guided tour on a miniature road train. Among the highlights are a golf course, safari park, a Byzantine fortress and a 1st-century Roman villa. There is also a museum, with stuffed animals on the ground floor and upstairs photos of Tito with his various visitors, including President Fidel Castro of Cuba and Queen Elizabeth II of Britain as well as film stars such as Richard Burton, Gina Lollobrigida and Sophia Loren. To explore the island in more depth, you can hire bicycles or electric golf carts, or even take a ride in Tito's 1953 Cadillac.

🔲 56 A2
🍴 Café (£) at harbour
📷 Boat trips from Fažana
➤ Pula (➤ 63), Vodnjan (➤ 67)

Boat trips

✉ Brijunska 10, Fažana
☎ 052 521880
🕐 Several times daily in summer, once or twice daily in winter
💰 Very expensive

> ### DID YOU KNOW?
>
> Most of the animals in the safari park are descendants of those presented to Tito by visiting heads of state. The two elephants, Sony and Lanka, were a gift from the Indian prime minister Indira Gandhi.

Tour boats ply back and forth to the Brijuni Islands

✚ 56 B3
🚌 Bus from Pula, Poreč and Rovinj
ℹ️ Trg Fontana 7
☎ 052 662343
► Hum (see below)

BUZET ✪✪

The largest of Istria's hill towns occupies a commanding position high above the River Mirna. The old town is a maze of cobbled streets and squares enclosed by medieval walls and gates. Buzet calls itself the 'city of truffles' and truffle-hunting is big business around here in autumn. Just along the Mirna Valley is Motovun (Montona), another hilltop town, with an attractive main square and splendid views from the ramparts.

✚ 56 A3
ℹ️ Umberta Gorjana 3
☎ 052 776349

Buzet, the largest of the Istrian hill towns

GROŽNJAN (GRISIGNANA) ✪✪✪

This charming hilltop village was deserted in the 1960s but has since been discovered by painters and musicians and is now a thriving artists' colony. Each year it becomes the venue for an international summer school of young musicians and concerts are held in the church on summer evenings. There are few specific sights but this is a lovely place to stroll, checking out the art galleries, sitting beneath the Venetian loggia and watching the sun set from the church terrace with distant views of the sea.

✚ 56 B3
► Buzet (see above)

HUM ✪✪

Hum's rather dubious claim to fame is that it is 'the smallest town in the world', with just 20 inhabitants but annual elections for mayor. In truth, it is just another village of stone houses but a very pretty one at that, with an excellent restaurant which justifies the visit. The road from Roč to Hum is known as Glagolitic Alley, and is lined with sculptures commemorating the Glagolitic script, a 41-letter Slavonic alphabet which was devised by Greek missionaries in the 9th century and used in religious texts in Croatia for a thousand years.

Istrian Hill Towns

This short circuit gives a good introduction to the scenery of inland Istria, and makes an easy half-day excursion from the coast.

Start in Buzet and follow signs to Buje along a beautiful road which runs through the Mirna Valley. After 18km (11 miles) you reach a crossroads where you turn left, crossing a bridge over the river on the way to Motovun.

The oldest part of Motovun is situated on top of the hill. You can leave your car in the car park at the bottom and walk up, or pay a toll in summer to drive up.

From Motovun continue on the same road in the direction of Pazin. When you reach a junction, turn left and follow signs into the centre of Pazin.

You could make a short break here to visit the castle and ethnographic museum (► 62).

Leave Pazin by taking the main road through the centre of town in the direction of Rijeka and the Učka tunnel. Ignore signs to the motorway and keep straight ahead on the old road to Rijeka, with the peak of Učka visible up ahead. After 8km (5 miles) you reach the village of Cerovlje.

Turn left here on the old road to Buzet, and left again at the next junction.

The road now starts to rise towards Draguć, one of the most dramatically situated of all the Istrian hill towns. Along the way there are spectacular views across central Istria, with the Ćićarija mountain ridge to your right.

Stay on this road to return to Buzet.

Distance
68km (42 miles)

Time
1.5 hours

Start/end point
Buzet

➕ 56 B3

Lunch
Hotel Kaštel (££)

✉ Trg Andrea Antico 7, Motovun
☎ 052 681607

Looking up towards Roč, another hill town to the east of Buzet

Mooring at Krk town

➕ 56 C2
🚌 Bus from Rijeka
⛴ Ferry from Cres and Rab
in summer
ℹ️ Trg Sveti Kvirina 1, Krk
town
☎ 051 221359
▶ Rab (▶ 64), Rijeka (▶ 64)

KRK ✪

Croatia's largest island is easily reached by a toll bridge south of Rijeka. The big draw here is Baška, at the island's southern tip, where one of Croatia's finest sandy beaches faces the Velebit mountains across the water. The capital, Krk town, was an old Roman city and you can still make out sections of the Roman walls. The neighbouring island of Cres is the second biggest in Croatia and features colonies of bottlenose dolphins and griffon vultures.

➕ 56 B2
🚌 Bus from Pula and Rijeka
ℹ️ Aldo Negri 20
☎ 052 855560

Labin National Museum
✉ Trg 1 Maja
☎ 052 852477
🕐 Mon–Fri 10–1, 5–7, Sat
10–1
✋ Moderate

LABIN (ALBONA) ✪✪

The southeast coast of Istria attracts far fewer visitors than the crowded resorts of the west. Just inland from the coast, Labin is an attractive hill town with an unspoilt medieval centre and a surprising coal-mining history. The main exhibit at the Labin National Museum is a reconstructed mine; visitors have to wear hard hats to stoop through its underground passages. Beneath Labin is Rabac, the only real resort on this stretch of coast, with several small beaches and coves around the harbour.

Viewpoint at Labin, with Rabac harbour in the distance

➕ 56 B3
🚌 Bus from Pula and Rijeka
ℹ️ Šetalište Maršala Tita 101
☎ 051 271710
▶ Rijeka (▶ 64)

OPATIJA ✪✪✪

At the turn of the 20th century Opatija was one of Europe's most fashionable resorts, a winter playground for the Austrian royals and Hapsburg aristocracy, who would while away their time in its casinos, ballrooms, villas, gardens and parks. It is still a popular resort, but these days the visitors are more likely to be Croatian honeymooners or weekenders. The grand *fin-de-siècle* villas and hotels still stand on the seafront, reminders of past glory, and the walk along the Lungomare (see facing page) still makes a delightful seaside stroll.

The Lungomare

This nostalgic walk follows the Lungomare (Italian for seafront), the popular name for the coastal path connecting Opatija with neighbouring beaches and towns. Begun in 1885 after the opening of the first hotels in Opatija, its full name is Šetalište Franz Josef I, after the Austro-Hungarian emperor of the time.

Start on the seafront in Opatija. The path is straightforward to follow as it clings to the shore in both directions.

The total length of the Lungomare is 12km (7 miles), running from Volosko, north of Opatija, to Lovran, south of Opatija.

The shorter stretch heads north from Opatija, passing the lush gardens of Villa Angiolina and Hotel Kvarner on its way out of town. Continue for around 4km (2 miles) to reach the fishing port of Volosko, with several excellent restaurants around the harbour.

Alternatively, you can head south from Opatija for 8km (5 miles) to Lovran. This is a lovely walk past elegant gardens and villas, palm, cypress and chestnut trees, and a rocky shoreline punctuated by pebble beaches. The promenade is lined with old-fashioned lamps and in places it forms arcades carved into the rock.

Passing the last cafés and ice-cream parlours, you leave Opatija behind. After 3km (2 miles) you reach Ičići, with a marina and beach. The path now continues to Ika, a small village with a terrace restaurant right on the beach.

Eventually, you reach Lovran, with its grand 19th-century villas. If you have the energy retrace your steps to Opatija; if not, there are regular buses.

Distance
8km (5 miles) each way, or 4km (2 miles) each way

Time
3 hours

Start point
Opatija

🗺 56 B3

End point
Lovran or Volosko

🗺 56 B2

Lunch
Ika (££)

✉ On the beach at Ika
☎ 051 291777

Outdoor dining at Volosko

🚌 56 B2

🚍 Bus from Pula, Poreč and Rovinj

ℹ️ Franine i Jurine 14

☎ 052 622460

Castle

✉️ Trg Istarskog Razvoda

🕐 Tue–Sun 10–6, mid-Apr–mid-Oct; Tue–Thu 10–3, Fri 12–5, Sat–Sun 11–5, mid-Oct–mid-Apr

✋ Moderate

🚌 56 A2

🚍 Bus from Pula, Rovinj and Vrsar

ℹ️ Zagrebačka 9

☎ 052 451293

► Vrsar (► 67)

Basilica of Euphrasius

✉️ Eufrazijeva

🕐 Daily 8–8 in summer, 10–7 in winter

✋ Free (museum and bell-tower: Inexpensive)

PAZIN (PISINO) ✪

This small town is actually the administrative capital of Istria, chosen because of its central position despite the size and importance of Pula. It is worth a short visit to see the castle, which contains the Istria Ethnographic Museum with displays of folk costumes and musical instruments, as well as a room devoted to Juraj Dobrila (1812–82), a local boy who rose to become bishop of Trieste and who is featured on the 10-kuna note.

The castle is situated on a cliff, overlooking a great gorge in the River Pazinčica which is said to have inspired the novelist Jules Verne (1828–1905)—the hero of his novel *Mathias Sandorf* was held prisoner in the castle and escaped by throwing himself into the pit.

POREČ (PARENZO) ✪✪✪

It would be easy to write off Poreč as an ugly example of mass tourism gone too far. This is, after all, Croatia's biggest resort, and the old Roman town is now completely dwarfed by the campsites, hotels and holiday complexes that have grown up around it. In summer, Poreč struggles to cope with an endless tide of visitors, yet at the heart of all this is a well-preserved old town containing one of Croatia's most remarkable sights—the 6th-century Basilica of Euphrasius with its extraordinary mosaics.

The first church on this site was built in the 4th century and dedicated to St Maur, a leader of the underground church who was martyred during the reign of the Roman emperor Diocletian. Some of the mosaics from the original church have survived, and can be seen through gaps in the floor. The real treasures, though, are the Byzantine mosaics in the central apse, richly encrusted with gold leaf. The upper panel depicts Christ with his apostles, while the central section features the Virgin Mary with the baby Jesus in her arms, surrounded by saints and angels including St Maur and Bishop Euphrasius holding a model of his basilica. Afterwards, you can climb the bell-tower and visit the museum of sacred art, in the bishop's palace just off the courtyard.

The old town makes for a pleasant stroll, with a pair of ruined Roman temples and narrow lanes leading off from the original main streets, Cardo and Decumanus. Boats leave from the harbour in summer for the wooded island of Sveti Nikola.

DID YOU KNOW?

The Irish author James Joyce lived in Pula briefly, working as an English teacher at the Berlitz language school in from 1904 to 1905. A bronze statue of Joyce sits on the terrace of the Uliks café, named after his novel *Ulysses* and situated beside the Arch of Sergi on the site of the old school.

PULA (POLA) ✪✪

Although the main reason for visiting Pula is to see the Roman arena (► 22), there are other interesting Roman sights in town. The 1st-century Temple of Augustus still stands on the edge of the old forum, now a pleasant café-lined square. Not far from here is the Arch of Sergi, erected by a wealthy Roman family in the 1st century BC in memory of a triumphant battle.

PULA ARENA (► 22, TOP TEN)

🚌 56 A1
🚌 Bus from Poreč and Rovinj
ℹ️ Forum 3
☎ 052 212987
► Brijuni Islands (► 57), Vodnjan (► 67)

Above: mosaics in the Euphrasius Basilica

RAB

The old Roman city of Arba, now known as Rab, is one of the Adriatic's most charming towns. With four tall Venetian bell-towers rising above the rooftops like the masts of a ship, it is at its best when seen from the sea. The old town is set on a narrow peninsula; you can climb a short section of the medieval walls for the best views.

The island of Rab has some excellent sandy beaches but is perhaps best known as the place where the British king Edward VIII bathed naked in 1936, one of the earliest recorded instances of naturism in Croatia.

RIJEKA

Croatia's biggest port has few major attractions, but many people find themselves here waiting to catch the ferry to Split or Dubrovnik. Among the grand Hapsburg-era buildings on the waterfront are the offices of the Jadrolinija ferry company, whose façade features reliefs and sculptures on nautical themes. Just back from the harbour, the Korzo is a busy shopping street and lively promenade. An archway beneath the clock tower leads to the oldest part of the city, dominated by the round cathedral of St Vitus.

ROVINJ (► 23, TOP TEN)

SENJ

If you are passing through on your way to the Plitvice Lakes (► 21), it is worth a brief stop in Senj to see the hilltop castle, the 16th-century power base of the feared Uskok warriors and pirates in their battles against the Ottoman Turks. A museum inside the castle tells the story of the Uskoks, along with costumes and weapons.

Rab's terracotta-tiled rooftops and bell-towers

The Leska Trail

The Nacionalni Park Risnjak occupies a large area of fir and beech forests in the Gorski Kotar mountain range, just inland from Rijeka. There are numerous challenging walks in the mountains, including a climb to the summit of Veliki Risnjak (1,528m/4,997ft), but this walk is designed to be done by anyone. You will need strong shoes and you should be prepared for cool weather—there could be snow on the ground for much of the year.

Start at the national park information office in the village of Crni Lug, signposted from the road from Rijeka to Delnice. Here you pay the park entrance fee and can pick up a leaflet about the walk.

The walk is well signposted, with a series of information panels in Croatian and English explaining the geology, landscapes and wildlife. This gives you a good introduction to the mountain scenery of the Gorski Kotar, with the minimum of effort. The educational trail takes in meadows and streams, as well as manmade features such as a charcoal kiln and a hamlet of wooden and stone cottages. There is also a feeding post for animals, with beds of hay where dormice and squirrels shelter during the winter. Bears, wolves, lynx and pine martens all live in these forests and can occasionally be spotted on moonlit nights.

Stay on the waymarked trail to return to the information office at Crni Lug.

The lodge here serves hearty mountain fare such as venison goulash, mushroom soup and trout from the River Kupa.

Distance
4.2km (2.6 miles)

Time
1.5 hours

Start point
Crni Lug

✚ 56 C3

Lunch
Motel Risnjak (££)

✉ Crni Lug
☎ 051 836133

On the Leska Trail (inset) in the Risnjak National Park (right)

🔢 56 A2
🚌 Bus from Pula
ℹ️ Svetvinčenat 96
☎️ 052 560005
► Pazin (► 62), Vodnjan (► 67)

SVETVINČENAT ⭐

If you are driving along the old road from Pula to Pazin, stop off to have a look at one of the most attractive town squares in Istria. To one side is the 13th-century castle of the Grimani family, with its high walls and towers. Also around the square are the parish church, town hall and Venetian loggia, completing a harmonious ensemble. The oldest building in town is the 12th-century Romanesque Church of St Vincent, whose walls are covered with frescoes. Like other towns in inland Istria, Svetvinčenat has a thriving arts scene and concerts are held in the castle courtyard in summer.

🔢 56 A3
🚌 Bus from Pula and Poreč
ℹ️ Obala Tita 3
☎️ 052 741363
► Grožnjan (► 58)

The tower of St Blaise in Vodnjan

UMAG ⭐

The northernmost resort on the Adriatic coast is just 40km (25 miles) from Trieste, making it popular with Italian visitors. In Croatia it is best known as the venue for the annual Croatia Open tennis tournament in late July. The old town, set on a narrow peninsula around a pretty bay, has almost been swallowed up by the tide of tourism around it. Savudrija, 8km (5 miles) north, is an attractive fishing port with pinewoods, rocky beaches

A never-ending task, on the shore of the Limski Kanal (a fjord)

and Croatia's oldest lighthouse, built in 1818, standing at right at the tip of the cape.

Just inland from Umag is the hilltop town of Buje, with a well-preserved medieval core and views from the ramparts to the sea.

VODNJAN (DIGNANO)

In the 18th century Vodnjan was larger than Pula but these days it is a modest country town with Venetian Gothic palaces and Renaissance townhouses lining its narrow streets and handsome main square. The parish Church of St Blaise dominates the town; at 63m (206ft), its bell-tower is the tallest in Istria. The collection of sacred art, behind the altar, includes the mummified remains of three saints brought here from Venice for safekeeping in 1818. So far there has been no scientific explanation as to how the bodies have managed to be preserved rather than decomposing, so inevitably they have been attributed with miraculous powers.

VRSAR AND LIMSKI KANAL

The coastal town of Vrsar (Orsera) was previously the summer residence of the bishops of Poreč and their castle still stands above the town. Another regular visitor was the Italian adventurer and legendary seducer Giacomo Casanova (1725–98), whose memoirs record conquests here. Vrsar stands at the mouth of the Limski Kanal, a 10km (6-mile) fjord situated between thickly wooded cliffs. Local tour operators offer boat trips through the fjord in summer, which usually include a fish picnic and a visit to a pirate cave.

🚹 56 A2
🚌 Bus from Pula
ℹ️ Narodni Trg 3
☎ 052 511672
► Brijuni Islands (►57), Pula (►63), Svetvinčenat (►66)

Sacred Art Collection
🕐 Daily 9–7 in summer
💰 Expensive

🚹 56 A2
🚌 Bus from Poreč and Rovinj
ℹ️ Rade Končara 46
☎ 052 441187
► Poreč (►62), Rovinj (►23)

67

Food & Drink

Croatian cooking is rooted in historical and geographical influences, and broadly divided into two distinct styles. The cuisine of the Adriatic coast is based on fresh fish and seafood, together with pasta and risotto, legacies of Italian and Venetian rule. By contrast, the cuisine of the continental regions is heavier and spicier, with dishes such as goulash betraying a central European influence.

Starters and Snacks

Almost every menu begins with *pršut* (cured ham, similar to an Italian prosciutto) and *paški sir* (sheep's cheese from the island of Pag), which together with bread and olives make the perfect starter. Pasta and risotto dishes are usually listed as 'warm starters'; a speciality is *crni rižot* (black risotto with cuttlefish ink). The popular national snack is *ćevapčići*, which is a kind of grilled meatball usually served with raw onions, *ajvar* (aubergine and pepper relish) and crusty bread. Alternatives include *pljeskavica* (hamburger) and *ražnjići* (kebabs). For a cheap snack, bakeries sell *burek* (filo pastry filled with minced meat or cheese).

Fresh fish can be found on the menu in every coastal village and town, and bread, cheese, olives and cured ham are also ubiquitous

Regional Specialities

In Istria, look out for local truffles, served in numerous ways but most commonly with steak, omelettes or pasta. Dalmatian dishes include *brodet* (fish casserole) and *pasticada* (beef stewed with sweet wine and served with gnocchi). Also popular along the coast is meat cooked under a *peka*, a metal lid which is covered with

hot embers. Specialities of the Zagorje, north of Zagreb, include *štrukli* (cottage cheese ravioli) and *purica z mlincima* (turkey with pasta).

The eastern region of Slavonia produces famously spicy food, such as *kulen* (paprika-flavoured salami), *gulaš* (goulash), *čobanec* (meat stew), *fiš paprikaš* (fish stew) and boiled beef with horseradish.

The mountain regions have their own cuisine, with hearty dishes reflecting the harsh climate. These include *grah* (bean stew with sausages), *janjetina* (spit-roast lamb) and game, which might be venison, wild boar or occasionally bear.

Main Courses

Grilled meat features on most menus, either as steak or schnitzels such as *zagrebački odrezak* (breaded veal stuffed with ham and cheese). Fish is usually plain grilled, and is often accompanied by *blitva* (spinach) and potatoes. Vegetables and salads are listed separately on the menu and generally include chips, rice, cabbage and beetroot salad.

Desserts

The most popular dessert is *palačinke* (pancakes filled with walnuts, chocolate or jam). Dalmatia produces *rožata*, which is similar to a *crème caramel*. The Croatians love *sladoled* (ice-cream), which is sold all over the country in a huge variety of flavours.

Wines, Beers and Spirits

Croatia produces some excellent wines. The best red wines are Dingač and Postup from the Pelješac Peninsula near Dubrovnik. White wines to look out for include Malvazija from Istria, Graševina from Slavonia, Grk and Pošip from Korčula and Vugava from Vis. *Prošek* is a sweet red wine from Dalmatia.

Lager-type beers include Karlovačko and Ožujsko. Strong brandy and spirits are often drunk either before or after a meal. The general term for these is *rakija*; popular varieties include *šlijivovica* (plum brandy), *lozovaca* (grape brandy), *travarica* (herb brandy) and *biska* (mistletoe brandy from Istria).

Croatian bottled beers and šlijivovica, a brandy made from plums

Dalmatia

Try to imagine the most alluring images of Croatia and you will probably be thinking of Dalmatia. From pine-fringed islands surrounded by turquoise seas to pretty little fishing ports and historic Venetian towns, Dalmatia has it all.

Travelling around the region is easy on the Magistrala coastal highway, or you can go island-hopping using the excellent network of ferries. The islands of Brač, Hvar and Korčula are justifiably popular but it is worth making the effort to seek out some of the more remote islands such as Vis and the Kornati archipelago.

Each of the towns and cities along the Dalmatian coast has its own particular appeal, but the undoubted highlight is Dubrovnik, a gem of a walled city that has risen from the ashes after being almost destroyed during the siege of 1991–2.

> *Those who seek paradise on earth should come to Dubrovnik*
>
> GEORGE BERNARD SHAW
> (1856–1950),
> *letter from Dubrovnik* (1929)

———————•———————

Dubrovnik's rooftops—21st-century style

Dubrovnik—Croatia's invincible golden city

Dubrovnik

Dubrovnik stands on a rocky peninsula, surrounded by its medieval walls. For 450 years this was the republic of Ragusa, a powerful maritime city-state that attracted the greatest artists, writers and architects of the time. Twice in its history, after the earthquake of 1667 and the siege of 1991–2, Dubrovnik has been threatened with extinction but each time it has recovered and been rebuilt. Dubrovnik today is once again a lively, prosperous city, enjoying a renaissance and a second golden age as Croatia's greatest tourist attraction.

What to See in Dubrovnik

➕ 75 D3
✉ Luža
🕐 Daily 8–12, 4.30–7
✋ Free

SVETOG VLAHA (CHURCH OF ST BLAISE) ✪
The city's favourite church is dedicated to St Blaise, a 3rd-century Armenian bishop who became Dubrovnik's patron saint after he appeared in a dream to a local priest to warn of a Venetian attack. His image can be seen all over the city, including the sculptures in the niches on the outsides of Pile and Ploče gates. The altar contains a gilded silver statue of St Blaise holding a model of pre-earthquake Dubrovnik.

➕ 75 D4
✉ Ulica Svetog Dominika
🕐 Daily 9–6 in summer, 9–3 in winter
✋ Inexpensive

DOMINIKANSKI SAMOSTAN ✪✪
(DOMINICAN MONASTERY)
The two great religious institutions of Dubrovnik were built at either end of the old town, inside the Pile and Ploče gates. This 15th-century monastery and cloister managed to survive the earthquake, though the bell-tower was added later. Highlights of the museum include an 11th-century Bible manuscript and a painting of Mary Magdalene by Titian, along with the sculpture of the Virgin and Child by Ivan Meštrović in the church.

FRANJEVAČKI SAMOSTAN (FRANCISCAN MONASTERY) ✪✪

Situated just off the Stradun inside the Pile Gate, the cool cloisters of the Franciscan monastery make a good place to escape the summer crowds and heat. Just off the cloisters is the former monastic dispensary, founded in 1317 and said to be the oldest continuously operating pharmacy in Europe. The museum contains an unexpected exhibit—a pair of Serbian shells which struck the monastery in 1991, preserved *in situ* beside the hole in the wall which they created. Also on display is *Novi Prsten* (New Ring), a charming double portrait of his wife by local artist Vlaho Bukovac (1855–1922).

74 B4
Stradun 2
Daily 9–6
Inexpensive

GRADSKE ZIDINE (CITY WALLS) (➤ 16, TOP TEN)

KATEDRALA (CATHEDRAL) ✪✪

The cathedral was built in 1713 after an earlier church on this site was destroyed in the earthquake. The attraction here is the grisly display of relics in the Treasury behind the altar. Many of them were fashioned by local craftsmen using the gold and silver filigree work for which Ragusa was famous. They include an enamelled gold skull case for the head of St Blaise, and richly jewelled reliquaries for the saint's arm and leg, which are paraded around the city on his feast day (3 February). Also here is a 16th-century silver chest, bizarrely said to contain Jesus' nappy.

75 D2
Pred Dvorom
Daily 8–8 in summer, Sat 8–5, Sun 11–5 in winter
Free (Treasury: inexpensive)

DID YOU KNOW?

The Ragusan republic had a reputation for religious tolerance which continues in Dubrovnik to this day. As well as numerous Catholic churches, within the city walls you can find a Serbian Orthodox church, a synagogue and a mosque. The small synagogue on Ulica Žudioska contains a Jewish Museum, with records of the Jewish community in Dubrovnik going back to the 15th century.

Entrance to the Franciscan Monastery

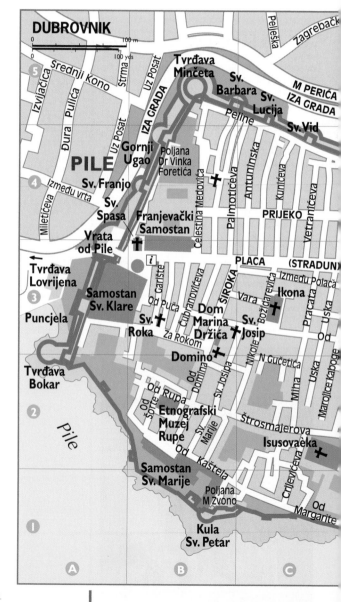

DUBROVNIK

0 ———————— 100 m
0 ———————— 100 yds

Tvrđava Minčeta

Sv. Barbara

Sv. Lucija

Sv. Vid

srednji kono

strma

Izvlačica

Dura Pulića

Izmedu vrta

Miletićeva

PILE

Uz Posat

Uz Posat

IZA GRADA

M PERIĆA

IZA GRADA

Pelline

Pelješka

Zagrebačk

Gornji Ugao

Poljana Dr Vinka Foretića

Celestina Medovića

Palmotićeva

Antuninska

Kunićeva

Vetranićeva

PRIJEKO

Sv. Franjo

Sv. Spasa

Franjevački Samostan

Vrata od Pile

Tvrđava Lovrijena

Samostan Sv. Klare

Puncjela

Tvrđava Bokar

Pile

Carište

Od Puča

Cubranovićeva

Za Rokom

PLACA   **(STRADUN)**

Izmedu Polača

SIROKA

vara

Božidarevića

Pracata

Uska

Od

Ikona

Dom Marina Držića

Sv. Josip

Sv. Roka

Domino

Nikole Gučetića

N Gučetića

Sv. Josipa

Miha

Uska

Uska

Marojice Kabage

Od Rupa

Od Sorte

Od Domina

Etnografski Muzej Rupe

Sv. Marije

Štrosmajerova

Chtileviceva

Isusovačka

Od Kaštela

Samostan Sv. Marije

Poljana M Zvono

Od Margarite

Kula Sv. Petar

A   **B**   **C**

5

4

3

2

1

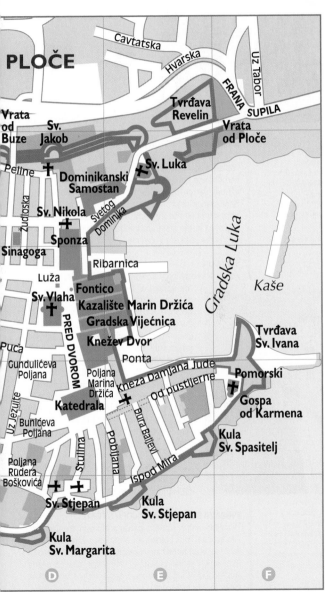

PLOČE

Cavtatska

Hvarska

Uz Tabor

FRANA SUPILA

Tvrđava Revelin

Vrata od Buze

Sv. Jakob

Vrata od Ploče

Peline

Sv. Luka

Dominikanski Samostan

Žudioska

Sv. Nikola

Svetog Dominika

Sponza

Sinagoga

Ribarnica

Gradska Luka

Kaše

Luža

Fontico

Sv. Vlaha

Kazalište Marin Držića

Gradska Vijećnica

PRED DVOROM

Knežev Dvor

Tvrđava Sv. Ivana

Puča

Ponta

Gundulićeva Poljana

Poljana Marina Držića

Kneza Damjana Jude

Pomorski

Od pustijerne

Uz Jezuite

Katedrala

Gospa od Karmena

Đura Baljevi

Bunićeva Poljana

Pobijana

Kula Sv. Spasitelj

Poljana Ruđera Boškovića

Stulina

Ispod Mira

Sv. Stjepan

Kula Sv. Stjepan

Kula Sv. Margarita

D

E

F

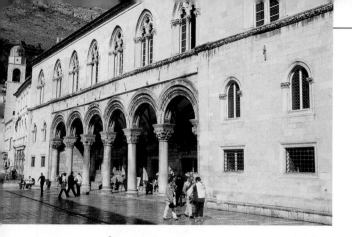

Above: the Rector's Palace
Below: the clock tower

74 C3

KNEŽEV DVOR (RECTOR'S PALACE) ⭐⭐

The Ragusan republic was governed by a Great Council of nobles, who would elect a rector (*knez*) from their number and confine him to this palace throughout his term of office, which lasted just one month. The Gothic-Renaissance palace now functions as the city museum, with portraits and furniture from Ragusa's golden age displayed in the state apartments. Classical concerts are held in the courtyard in summer.

STRADUN ⭐⭐⭐

For all its magnificent architecture and churches, much of the appeal of Dubrovnik lies in sitting at outdoor cafés soaking up the street life. Nowhere is better for doing this than Stradun, the central promenade of the walled town. Once lined with Gothic palaces, Stradun was rebuilt after the earthquake and this is what gives it such a harmonious feel, with identical three-storey houses with arched doorways and green shutters. So many people have walked this street that the flagstones have been polished to a sheen by passing feet. Stradun runs in a straight line from Vrata od Pile (Pile Gate) to the clock tower on Luža Square. From here, a gate leads to the Gradska Luka (Old Port), once busy with maritime activity but now a pleasure harbour, with a café in the former arsenal and boats leaving for Cavtat (▶ 78) and Lokrum (▶ 78).

TVRDAVA SVETI IVANA (ST JOHN'S FORT) ⭐

This 16th-century fortress stands guard over the Old Port. The ground floor houses an aquarium, while the upper floor has been turned into a maritime museum devoted to Dubrovnik's seafaring history, with maps, nautical charts and models of argosies—the merchant ships which took their name from Ragusa.

Dubrovnik Old Town

Cars are not allowed inside the old city, making it perfect for walking. Most local buses stop outside Pile Gate, the obvious starting-point for a walk.

Cross the stone bridge and a wooden drawbridge to reach the outer gate, topped by a statue of St Blaise. Pass through the inner gate, also sporting an effigy of the saint, to arrive on Stradun.

To your right is the large Onofrio Fountain, built in 1444.

Walk straight ahead along Stradun and take the first right, passing beneath an archway into Ulica Gariste. Turn left at the crossroads into Ulica Od Puča.

This is the main shopping street of the old town, with several art galleries and jewellery shops.

Continue to the end of the street to arrive in Gundulićeva Poljana, scene of a lively morning market. Keep straight on across the square to emerge in front of the Rector's Palace. Turn left to return to Stradun beneath the clock tower.

The Gradska Kavana café makes a good place to take in the atmosphere, with one terrace facing Stradun and another facing the Old Port.

Turn left along Stradun and take the second right onto Ulica Žudioska, at the heart of the old Jewish ghetto. Climb the steps past the synagogue to reach Prijeko.

This busy street, parallel to Stradun, has many tourist-oriented restaurants.

Keep climbing to arrive on Peline, the highest street of the old town. Turn left and follow this lane inside the medieval walls. Just before reaching the Minčeta Tower, turn left along Palmotićeva and take the steep steps downhill to return to Stradun near the Pile Gate.

Distance
1km (0.6 mile)

Time
1 hour

Start point
Vrata od Pile (Pile Gate)

🚏 74 A3

🚌 1A, 1B, 2, 3, 4, 5, 6, 8, 9

Lunch
Kamenice (££)

📍 Poljana Gundulićeva 8
☎ 020 323682

The Onofrio Fountain: water pours out from masks around its sides

What to See Around Dubrovnik

81 F1
Bus 10 from Dubrovnik
Boat from Dubrovnik
Tiha 3
020 479025

CAVTAT ◐◐

Conveniently situated just a few kilometres from the airport, Cavtat is much the most attractive of the so-called Dubrovnik Riviera resorts. With regular taxi-boats in summer to Dubrovnik's Old Port, it makes the perfect base for anyone looking to combine a beach holiday with a city break. Two sheltered bays are divided by a wooded

promontory, with a palm-lined promenade and seafront paths leading to sand and pebble beaches. A path leads to the summit of the peninsula, where the cemetery contains a domed mausoleum designed for a local family by Ivan Meštrović. This was the site of the Greek colony of Epidaurum, one of the first settlements in Croatia in the 3rd century BC, pre-dating Dubrovnik by a thousand years.

Cavtat's quayside

Cavtat is the main town of the Konavle region, a fertile strip of farmland which extends to the border with Montenegro. The people of the Konavle are known for their colourful costumes, and folklore performances are held on Sunday mornings in summer in the nearby village of Čilipi.

81 E1
Ferry from Dubrovnik
Lopud
020 759086

ELAFITSKI OTOCI (ELAFITI ISLANDS) ◐◐

The peaceful, traffic-free isles of Koločep, Lopud and Šipan have long provided relaxing retreats for the people of Dubrovnik. There are few permanent residents, but many people have summer homes here and tourism is an important source of income. Besides walking among orchards, gardens and vineyards, the main draws are the easygoing pace of life and the many secluded beaches and coves. The best sandy beach is at Šunj on Lopud. You can visit the islands by ferry from Gruž harbour or by shuttle boats from Dubrovnik's Old Port.

81 F1
Café (£) near harbour; restaurant (££) in monastery in summer
Boat from Dubrovnik
Boat trip: expensive

LOKRUM ◐◐◐

If you only make one trip out of Dubrovnik, it should be to the wooded isle of Lokrum, which is clearly visible just offshore as you walk around the city walls. Boats depart regularly in summer from the Old Port, and the journey takes just 15 minutes. For the people of Dubrovnik, Lokrum is a garden of Eden, a place of legendary beauty

En route to the French fort on Lokrum

The grotto and carp pool in the Trsteno Arboretum

where they go to escape the summer heat by strolling through its gardens and relaxing on its beaches. One early visitor was the English king Richard the Lionheart (1157–99), who is said to have been shipwrecked here on his way back from the Crusades and to have built a cathedral in Dubrovnik to give thanks for his survival. Much later, in 1806, the French built a fortress on the summit of the island; you can climb onto the roof for panoramic views.

A short walk from the harbour leads to an abandoned Benedictine monastery, with cloisters and formal gardens. The nearby Mrtvo More (Dead Sea) saltwater lake has good swimming, though many people prefer the island's popular nudist beach.

TRSTENO ARBORETUM ✪
The gardens at Trsteno are a rare survivor from the days of the Ragusan republic, when statesmen and aristocrats would retire in summer to their Renaissance villas outside the city. Laid out in the 16th century, the gardens make a lovely place to stroll, with shady avenues and an ornamental grotto flanked by statues of nymphs. A path leads down to Trsteno's harbour, with dreamy views of the Elafiti Islands across the water.

➕ 81 E1
✉ Trsteno, 24km (15 miles) north of Dubrovnik
☎ 020 751019
🕐 Daily 8–8 in summer, 8–5 in winter
🚌 Bus from Dubrovnik
💶 Moderate

DALMATIA

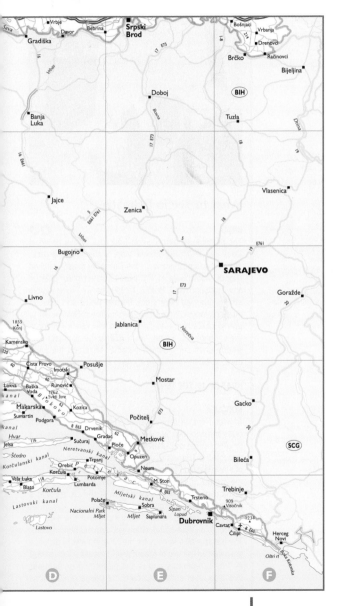

Vrbje
Gradiška
Davor
Bebrina
Srpski Brod
Bošnjaci
Vrbanja
Drenovci
Brčko
Računovci
Bijeljina

Doboj
BIH

Banja Luka
Tuzla

Jajce
Zenica
Vlasenica

Bugojno
SARAJEVO
Goražde

Livno
Jablanica
BIH

1855 Konj
Kamensko
Cista Provo
Posušje
Imotski
Mostar

Lokva
Baška Voda
Runović
1762 Sveti Jure
Kozica
Gacko

Makarska
Sumartin
Podgora
Drvenik
Počitelj

Hvar
Jelsa
Sučuraj
Gradac
Ploče
Metković
Opuzen
Neum

Šćedro
Korčulanski kanal
Orebić
Trpanj
Bileća

Vela Luka
Blato
Korčula
Lumbarda
Potomje
M. Ston
Trebinje

Lastovski kanal
Polače
Mljetski kanal
Sobra
Šipan
Lopud
Trsteno
909 Višočnik

Lastovo
Nacionalni Park Mljet
Mljet
Saplunara
Dubrovnik
Cavtat
Ćilipi
Herceg Novi

Oštri rt

SCG

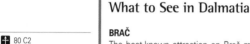

*Korčula's old town gate
on the landward side*

80 C2
Ferry from Split or
Makarska

Polat Bolskih Pomoraca,
Bol

021 635638

► Hvar (► 19), Zlatni Rat
(► 26)

What to See in Dalmatia

BRAČ ✪✪
The best-known attraction on Brač may be the beach at
Zlatni Rat (► 26), but there is more to the island than that.
This is the largest island off the Dalmatian coast, watched
over by Vidova Gora, at 778m (2,544ft) the highest peak on
any Croatian island. Brač is famous for its white marble
stone, quarried here since Roman times and used in
buildings ranging from Diocletian's palace in Split (► 86) to
Liverpool Cathedral in the UK and the White House in
Washington DC. Ferries from Split arrive at Supetar, a
sleepy town set around a harbour. Milna, on the west
coast, is another attractive village in a sheltered bay.

HVAR (► 19, TOP TEN)

81 D1
Bus from Dubrovnik

Ferry from Dubrovnik or
Orebić

Obala Franje Tuđmana

020 715701

► Pelješac (► 84)

KORČULA ✪✪✪
Crowded onto a narrow peninsula with the sea on three
sides and enclosed by medieval walls, Korčula resembles a
smaller version of Dubrovnik. The entry to the old town is
through the 15th-century Land Gate, where a broad flight
of steps leads up to an archway crowned by a winged lion,
the symbol of Venice. From here, you plunge into a maze
of narrow lanes with a cathedral at the centre and a
promenade leading around the outer walls.

Korčula claims to be the birthplace of the explorer
Marco Polo (1254–1324), who was captured here in 1298.
The island is also famous for the Moreška sword dance, a
good-versus-evil tale of Moors and Christians which arrived
in the 16th century and is still performed on summer
evenings. Just outside Korčula, the village of Lumbarda
has vineyards and a sandy beach.

KORNATI OTOCI (KORNATI ISLANDS) ✪✪✪

This archipelago of more than 100 rocky islands, including Kornati and Murter, off the north Dalmatian coast is a paradise for sailors, with calm seas, crystal-clear waters and a remote, ethereal beauty. The Irish playwright George Bernard Shaw (1856–1950) wrote that when the gods wanted to crown their work, on the last day they created Kornati 'from their tears, the stars and their breath'.

For much of the year the islands are uninhabited but in summer the residents of Murter, owners of most of the land, set up fish restaurants for visiting yachtsmen and rent out old fishermen's cottages for a 'Robinson Crusoe' experience, with no electricity, water from a well and supplies delivered by boat. For a shorter visit, travel agents in Murter, Zadar and Šibenik offer regular full-day excursions in summer.

- 🔳 80 B3
- 🚢 Boat trips from Murter, Zadar and Šibenik
- ► Šibenik (► 85), Zadar (► 89)

Nacionalni Park Kornati

- ℹ️ Ulica Butina 2, Murter
- ☎ 022 434662
- 💵 Expensive (included in cost of boat excursion)

NACIONALNI PARK KRKA ✪✪✪

The gorges and waterfalls of the River Krka rival the Plitvice Lakes (► 21) for their beauty, and are much easier to visit if you are staying on the Dalmatian coast. The highlight is Skradinski Buk, a 45m (147-ft) series of cascades tumbling into a pool where people go swimming in summer. From the top of the waterfall, boat trips make the journey along a wooded canyon to the islet of Visovac, home to a Franciscan monastery founded in 1445. Some of the trips continue to a second waterfall at Roški Slap. Even without the boat trip, it is worth visiting the park to walk around the waterfall at Skradinski Buk. You can get there by national park boat from the village of Skradin, or shuttle bus from Lozovac.

- 🔳 80 B3
- ✉️ 12km (7 miles) north of Šibenik
- ☎ 022 217720
- 🕐 Daily 8–8 in summer, 8–5 in winter
- 🍴 Cafés (£) at Skradinski Buk and Roški Slap
- 🚌 Bus from Šibenik
- 💵 Expensive
- ► Šibenik (► 85)

The Skradinski Buk falls in the Krka National Park

MAKARSKA RIVIJERA ✪

+ 81 D2
🚌 Bus from Split and Dubrovnik
ℹ️ Obala Kralja Tomislava, Makarska
☎ 021 612002
► Brač (► 82), Split (► 86)

From Brela in the north to Gradac in the south, the Makarska riviera is a 60km (37-mile) stretch of coastal resorts linked by the Magistrala highway. Apart from the west coast of Istria, this is the most intensively developed area of tourism in Croatia, and the towns along this strip lack the history and character of places such as Dubrovnik and Korčula. Nevertheless, former fishing villages like Brela and Baška Voda retain a fair amount of charm, and there are some excellent white-pebble beaches at Brela, Makarska and Tučepi. The coastline is overlooked by the Biokovo table mountain (1,762m/5,762ft), the second highest in Croatia.

MLJET (► 20, TOP TEN)

PELJEŠAC ✪✪

+ 81 D2
🚌 Bus from Dubrovnik and Korčula
⛴️ Ferry from Korčula to Orebić
ℹ️ Trg Mimbeli, Orebić
☎ 020 713718
► Korčula (► 82)

The Pelješac Peninsula is connected to the mainland by a narrow isthmus at Ston. The village of Mali Ston is known for its oysters, while the twin town of Veli Ston is still enclosed by its 14th-century walls. A 90km (56-mile) road crosses the peninsula, climbing high above the coast with views to Korčula, Mljet and Vis. The road passes through the Potomje vineyards, famous throughout Croatia for Dingač, the country's most expensive red wine.

The Markarska riviera with the Biokovo massif in the background

NACIONALNI PARK PLITVIčKA JEZERA (► 21, TOP TEN)

SALONA ✪✪

+ 80 C2
✉ 5km (3 miles) from Split
☎ 021 212900
🕐 Daily 7–7 in summer, Mon–Fri 7–7, Sat 10–7, Sun 4–7 in winter
🍴 Café (£)
🚌 Bus from Split
💷 Inexpensive
► Split (► 86), Trogir (► 88)

Two thousand years ago, when Split was no more than a fishing village, Salona was the richest city on the coast, a thriving town of 60,000 people and the birthplace of the Roman emperor Diocletian. The city has long been

> ### DID YOU KNOW?
>
> The coast road from Split to Dubrovnik passes briefly through Bosnia-Herzegovina at the border town of Neum. You will need to show your passport but you should not have any problem getting through. The only way to avoid it is by taking the ferry from Ploče to Trpanj on the Pelješac Peninsula.

Statue of George the Dalmation, outside Šibenik cathedral

abandoned, but you can get some sense of its scope by wandering around the ruins. Half-hidden among the fields is the Roman amphitheatre, where gladiatorial contests were held in front of a crowd of 15,000 spectators. Domnius, the first bishop of Salona, was executed in the theatre in AD 304 and his tomb can be seen in the ruins of a basilica. There is a small archaeological museum on site, but most of the finds from Salona are in the Archaeological Museum at Split (► 86).

All that remains of the amphitheatre at Salona

ŠIBENIK ☻☻

Šibenik stands in a sheltered harbour at the mouth of the River Krka. Although it is now a sprawling industrial city, like so many towns on this coast it has a compact old town at its core. The biggest draw is the cathedral, designed by Juraj Dalmatinac (George the Dalmatian, c1400–73), whose statue, by Ivan Meštrović, stands outside. This is probably the finest example of Venetian Gothic architecture in Croatia, full of delicately carved stonework both inside and out. The most enjoyable feature of the cathedral is the frieze of 74 stone heads running around the exterior of the apses; they are thought to be unflattering portraits of local citizens who refused to pay towards the cost of the building.

✚ 80 B3
🚌 Bus from Split, Trogir and Zadar
ℹ️ Obala Dr Franje Tu mana 5
☎ 022 214448
► Kornati Otoci (► 83), Nacionalni Park Krka (► 83)

Split

Croatia's second city is the source of much regional pride, enjoying a fierce rivalry with Zagreb in everything from fashion to football. This is a modern, bustling port city and the hub of the Dalmatian ferry network with boats leaving for Brač, Hvar, Korčula and Vis. Street life centres on the waterfront Riva, crowded with open-air cafés. The main sights are situated around Diocletian's Palace (►24) and on the Marjan Peninsula to the west.

What to See in Split

🔢 80 C2
✉ Zrinsko-Frankopanska 25
☎ 021 318720
🕐 Tue–Fri 9–noon, 5–8, Sat and Sun 9–1, Jun–Sep; Tue–Fri 9–2, Sat and Sun 9–1, Oct–May
🎫 Inexpensive

The Iron Gate—one of four—into the old town centre: the others are named Golden, Silver and Bronze

ARHEOLOŠKI MUZEJ   ✪✪
(ARCHAEOLOGICAL MUSEUM)

Croatia's oldest museum, founded in 1820, features objects excavated from the Roman city at Salona (►84). Among the items on display are jewellery, pottery, glass jars, coins and a 2nd-century mosaic of the god Apollo. Also here are ancient Greek artefacts from the island of Vis, including wine jars and a beautiful clay oil lamp depicting the gods Isis and Serapis. Be sure to leave time for a walk around the semi-circular courtyard gallery, which contains numerous examples of Roman art, with mosaics and sarcophagi featuring scenes of everyday life such as chariot racing, hunting and bunches of grapes.

DIOKLECIJANOVE PALAČE (DIOCLETIAN'S PALACE)
(►24, TOP TEN)

🔢 80 C2
✉ Narodni Trg 1
☎ 021 344164
🕐 Mon–Fri 10–3
🎫 Inexpensive

ETNOGRAFSKI MUZEJ   ✪✪
(ETHNOGRAPHIC MUSEUM)

Housed in the 15th-century town hall just outside the walls of Diocletian's palace, this enjoyable museum features traditional folk costumes from both coastal and inland Dalmatia. Among the displays are cavalry uniforms, fur hats, swords and lances from the Sinjska Alka, an annual festival of jousting and horsemanship held in the nearby town of Sinj each August to commemorate a victory over the Ottoman Turks in 1715.

GALERIJA MEŠTROVIĆ ✪✪

The sculptor Ivan Meštrović spent much of his childhood in Dalmatia and he planned this grand villa as his summer-house and studio, though he only lived here for two years before spending the rest of his life in exile in the United States. The house and garden contain a representative collection of his work, including female nudes, family portraits and religious studies. The ticket also includes entry to the nearby Kaštelet, a 16th-century chapel bought by Meštrović to house his *Life of Christ* cycle.

➕ 80 C2
✉ Šetalište Ivana Meštrovića 46
☎ 021 340800
🕐 Tue–Sun 9–9, May–Sep; Tue–Sat 9–4, Sun 10–3, Oct–Apr
🚌 Bus 12
💲 Moderate

KATEDRALA (CATHEDRAL) ✪✪✪

Situated in the central peristyle court of Diocletian's palace and guarded by a black granite sphinx from Egypt, the octagonal temple designed as the emperor's mausoleum was later turned into the city's cathedral. Look carefully into the dome and you can still make out reliefs of chariot races from Roman times, together with portraits of Diocletian and his wife. The cathedral is full of symbolism—the pulpit was carved out of stone from Diocletian's tomb and there are altars to two bishops martyred by Diocletian. You can climb the separate bell-tower for views over the city.

➕ 80 C2
✉ Peristil
🕐 Mon–Sat 8–12, 4–7; daily 8–7 Jul–Sep
💲 Inexpensive

MARJAN ✪✪

Climb the steps on Senjska at the west end of the Riva to reach the Marjan Peninsula, a cool green hill overlooking the city. This is where people come to escape the summer heat, with shady woodland walks, ancient hermitage chapels and peaceful views out to sea. The café terrace at the top of the steps is a popular lookout point. A path from here leads to the summit.

➕ 80 C2
🍴 Caffe Vidilica (£)

The arcaded Town Hall on Narodni Trg

📍 80 C2
🚌 Bus 37 from Split
ℹ️ Trg Ivana Pavla II
☎️ 021 881412
▶ Salona (▶ 84), Split (▶ 86)

TROGIR ✪✪✪

Built on a small island and connected by bridges to the mainland and the larger island of Čiovo, Trogir is one of the most attractive towns on the Adriatic coast. It is possible to walk right around the island in under half an hour, but you could easily spend all day getting lost in its narrow streets. The main sight is the cathedral, begun in the 13th century but topped by a distinctive three-storey Venetian campanile, which was completed three centuries later.

The most remarkable feature is the west portal, carved in 1240 and richly illustrated with depictions of everyday farming life including the grape harvest and the annual pig slaughter, together with more conventional angels, saints and scenes from the life of Christ. Inside the cathedral, the greatest treasure is the 15th-century vaulted chapel of St John.

Across the square is the Venetian loggia, also dating from the 15th century. Much of the action takes place on the Riva, the waterfront promenade, with its numerous cafés and bars. At the west end of the Riva, the Kamerlengo fortress was built as the residence of the Venetian governor; you can climb the tower and stroll around the battlements for views over the town.

Trogir's picturesque waterfront

VIS ⊛⊛

This remote Adriatic island was first settled by the ancient Greeks, who founded the town of Issa in the 4th century BC. Until 1989, however, Vis was off limits to foreign tourists due to its strategic military importance. During World War II Tito established his base on the island in a cave on Mount Hum, where he held secret meetings with British diplomats and spies. The British connection with Vis goes back much further; the island was occupied by British troops during the Napoleonic wars (1811–15) and it still has a cricket club today. A path on the west side of the harbour climbs to the ruined George III fortress, with a carved Union Jack (British flag) above the door. Across the bay is a small English cemetery, with memorials to the dead of the 19th century and 'Tito's liberation war'.

St Donat's Church tower, in Zadar

🚩 80 C2
⛴ Ferry from Split
ℹ Šetalište Stare Isse 5
☎ 021 717017

Today, Vis is a laid-back island of vineyards and fishing ports, popular with visiting sailors. In recent years it has developed an increasingly chic reputation, and there are several expensive fish restaurants by the harbours in both Vis town and Komiža. In summer you can take a boat trip from Komiža to the neighbouring island of Biševo, entering a natural grotto known as the Modra Špilja (Blue Cave).

ZADAR ⊛⊛

The major city of northern Dalmatia is built on a peninsula, still partly enclosed by its medieval walls. After suffering heavy bombardment during World War II, Zadar is a strange mix of old and new. At the heart of it all is the old Roman forum, the stone from which was used to build St Donat's Church, a 9th-century Byzantine round church dedicated to an Irish bishop. Some 20km (12 miles) north of Zadar, the island village of Nin was once Croatia's ecclesiastical capital and it contains one of the country's greatest treasures, the tiny, whitewashed 9th-century chapel known as the Cathedral of the Holy Cross.

🚩 80 A3
🚌 Bus from Šibenik and Split
⛴ Ferry from Rijeka, Split and Dubrovnik
ℹ Narodni Trg 5
☎ 023 316166
➤ Kornati Otoci (► 83)

ZLATNI RAT, BRAČ (► 26, TOP TEN)

Through the Krajina

Distance
230km (142 miles)

Time
5 hours

Start/end point
Zadar

➕ 80 A3

Lunch
Ankora (££)

✉ Tvrđava (inside the fortress at Knin)

☎ 022 662996

This long drive takes you through the Krajina, the historic border region occupied by Serbs living in Croatia. During the war of 1991–5, rebel Serbs declared the Republic of the Serbian Krajina at Knin. After the war, most of the Serbs fled into Bosnia, leaving many villages abandoned. The scars of war are still visible in the ruins of bombed-out houses.

Follow the coast road south for 70km (43 miles) from Zadar to Šibenik, with the mountains on your left and the islands of the Zadar and Kornati archipelagos to your right. On the outskirts of Šibenik, after crossing the bridge over the River Krka, turn left towards Drniš. Pass the turn-off for the Krka National Park and continue ahead with the Dinaric Mountains on the horizon.

The road climbs to the head of a gorge where you will see the ruined castle above Drniš.

Turn right at Drniš and follow the railway line to Knin.

The town is dominated by its fortress, previously in rebel hands, now symbolically flying the Croatian flag.

Flying the flag (➤ 7)

Drive through Knin and turn left at the roundabout towards Zagreb. The road climbs onto a plateau. After 7km (4 miles), turn left towards Benkovac. In the village of Kistanje, turn right, signposted to Obrovac. Keep right when the road forks and stay on this road across a bleak landscape of deserted villages.

When you reach a junction, Obrovac is hidden in the gorge to your right, on the Zrmanja river.

Turn left here and stay on this long straight road to return to Zadar.

Where To...

NACIONALNI PARK "PAKLENICA"

ULAZ ENTRANCE 500 m

Above: lavender products are everywhere in Hvar

Zagreb

Prices

Prices are approximate, based on a three-course meal for one without drinks and service:

£ = under 100kn
££ = 100kn–150kn
£££ = over 150kn

Fresh fish is sold by weight and usually works out to be quite expensive. Salads, vegetables and side dishes generally have to be ordered separately.

Baltazar (££)

Traditional restaurant specializing in grilled meat in a courtyard near the cathedral. If you have a Zagreb Card, you get a 20 per cent discount.

⊠ Nova Ves 4
☎ 01 466 6824
🕔 Mon–Sat 12–12

Boban (££)

Trendy Italian cellar restaurant and bar in a pedestrian street just off Trg Bana Jelačića.

⊠ Ulica Ljudevita Gaja 9
☎ 01 481 1549
🕔 Daily 11am–midnight

K Pivovari (££)

Rustic food and a great choice of beers at a pub attached to Zagreb's oldest brewery. Steaks, sausages and baked potatoes washed down with Ožujsko or Tomislav beer.

⊠ Ilica 222
☎ 01 375 1808
🕔 Mon–Sat 10am–midnight, Sun 10–5

Kamenita Vrata (£)

Popular pizzeria frequented by students and tourists, just inside the Stone Gate in Gornji Grad. A good choice for a snack lunch while exploring the upper town.

⊠ Ulica Kamenita 5
☎ 01 482 9111
🕔 Daily 10am–11pm

Kerempuh (££)

Busy restaurant on the upper level of Dolac market, offering fresh produce from the market stalls below. Get here early for a seat on the terrace.

⊠ Dolac market
☎ 01 481 9000
🕔 Mon–Sat 6–3, 5–midnight

Paviljon (£££)

Refined menu of Italian and Central European cuisine in the ornate cream-coloured Art Pavilion, built in 1896 in a park opposite the railway station.

⊠ Trg Kralja Tomislava 22
☎ 01 481 3066
🕔 Mon–Sat 12–12

Pod Gričkim Topom (££)

Romantic restaurant serving grilled meat and fish dishes and traditional Croatian cuisine on a flower-filled terrace overlooking the city from Gornji Grad.

⊠ Zakmardijeve Stuve 5 (beside upper funicular terminus)
☎ 01 483 3607
🕔 Daily 11am–midnight

Rubelj (£)

One of several down-to-earth grills on a terrace beneath Dolac market, offering a simple but delicious range of ćevapčići and kebabs served in huge crusty baps.

⊠ Dolac 2
☎ 01 481 8777
🕔 Daily 8am–11pm

Vallis Aurea (£)

Spicy Slavonian home cooking at decent prices, in a cosy tavern with wooden tables near the foot of the funicular to Gornji Grad.

⊠ Ulica Tomića 4
☎ 01 483 1305
🕔 Mon–Sat 9am–11pm

Vincek (£)

Delicious cakes and pastries and wonderful ice-creams at this popular slastičarnica near Trg Bana Jelačića.

⊠ Ilica 18
☎ 01 483 3612
🕔 Daily 9am–11pm

Inland Croatia

Đakovo
Rio (£)
If you're tired of heavy Slavonian stews, this pizzeria just off the main promenade serves pizzas and pasta in a brick-arched dining-room and on a summer terrace.

✉ Ulica Hrvatskih Velikana 5
☎ 031 820176
🕐 Daily 8am–11pm

Kopački Rit
Kod Varge (£)
Fiery *kulen* (salami), *fiš paprikaš* (fish casserole) and fried carp from local rivers are the specialities at this family-run tavern in the village of Bilje.

✉ Ulica Kralja Zvonimira 37A, Bilje
☎ 031 750120
🕐 Daily 8am–11pm

Osijek
Slavonska Kuča (££)
Cosy little place on the edge of the Tvrđa fortress, serving typically spicy Slavonian country cooking such as *čobanec*, a meat stew flavoured with paprika.

✉ Ulica Firingera 26
☎ 031 208277
🕐 Mon–Sat 9am–11pm

Samobor
Kavana Livadić (£)
The best of the Viennese-style pastry shops around Samobor's main square, offering tempting treats such as *samoborska kremšnita* (custard tart).

✉ Trg Kralja Tomislava 1
☎ 01 336 5850
🕐 Daily 8am–11pm

Pri Staroj Vuri (££)
Smart, traditional restaurant in a mustard-coloured townhouse behind the church, specializing in grilled meat and fish dishes from the days of the Hapsburg empire.

✉ Ulica Giznik 2
☎ 01 336 0548
🕐 Mon–Sat 11–11, Sun 11–6

Samoborska Pivnica (££)
Cavernous beer hall set just back from the main square, with an emphasis on simple meat dishes such as beef tongue and local sausages served with strong Samobor mustard.

✉ Šmidhenova 3
☎ 01 336 1623
🕐 Daily 9am–11pm

Varaždin
Park (££)
Grilled meat dishes and daily lunchtime specials on a large summer terrace overlooking the city's main park – perfectly placed for a stroll to walk off your meal.

✉ Habdelićeva 6
☎ 042 211467
🕐 Mon–Sat 9am–11pm, Sun 10–10

Zlatna Guška (£££)
Relive the days of the Austro-Hungarian empire in this atmospheric cellar restaurant, with pikestaffs on the walls and ancient recipes such as beef daggers and nettle soup.

✉ Habdelićeva 4
☎ 042 213393
🕐 Daily 9am–11pm

Zagorje
Grešna Gorica (£)
Farmhouse restaurant offering rustic casseroles and game dishes such as venison goulash, on a terrace with views to Veliki Tabor.

✉ Taborgradska 3, Desinić
☎ 049 343001
🕐 Daily 10–10

Eating Out in Croatia
Typical mealtimes are 12–3 for lunch and 7–10 for dinner, but most restaurants stay open throughout the day. Booking is rarely necessary, though many places close on Sundays and reduce their hours in winter, so it is worth checking in advance. Most restaurants feature a standard menu of Croatian and international cuisine, though a *konoba* or *gostionica* is more likely to serve regional fare. A *slastičarnica* is a pastry-shop, also specializing in *sladoled* (ice-cream).

Istria and Kvarner Bay

Truffles

These powerfully scented tubers are found in the oak woods around Buzet and Motovun in autumn. The best white truffles can fetch up to 20,000 kuna per kilo, but if you can't afford those prices, local restaurants throughout Istria offer pasta, steaks and omelettes flavoured with thinly sliced or grated truffles. A word of warning—truffles are renowned for their aphrodisiac qualities.

Buzet

Toklarija (£££)

One of the most expensive restaurants in Croatia serves top-quality Istrian produce in a restored oil mill above the Mirna Valley. Booking essential.

🖂 Sovinjsko Polje 11 (off the main road from Buzet to Motovun)

☎ 052 663031

⌚ Wed–Mon 1–10

Hum

Humska Konoba (££)

Small, rustic tavern in the tiny village of Hum, serving hearty dishes of pasta, truffles, goulash and roast lamb. A speciality is the home-made *biska* (mistletoe brandy).

🖂 Hum 2

☎ 052 660005

⌚ Daily 11–10, Jun–Oct; weekends only, Nov–May

Motovun

Barbacan (£££)

Cool, Italian-style bistro just outside the town gates, with stone walls, candlelit tables and a menu featuring creative truffle dishes.

🖂 Ulica Barbacan 1

☎ 052 681791

⌚ Lunch and dinner Tue–Sun, Mar–Nov

Enoteka Zigante (£££)

The flagship restaurant of the Zigante Tartufi truffle empire is found in the village of Livade. Not surprisingly, truffles appear on the menu in various guises.

🖂 Livade 7

☎ 052 664302

⌚ Thu–Tue 12–11

Kaštel (££)

Generous portions of inland Istrian cuisine, such as pasta, goulash or steak with truffles, beneath the chestnut trees on the main square in summer.

🖂 Trg Andrea Antico 7

☎ 052 681607

⌚ Daily 8am–10pm

Pod Voltom (££)

Brick-vaulted cellar beneath the arches at the entrance to the main square, specializing in fresh truffles in season, served with omelette, veal medallions or steak.

🖂 Trg Josefa Ressela

☎ 052 681923

⌚ Thu–Tue 12–12 in summer, 12–9 in winter

Opatija

Bevanda Lido (£££)

Smart fish and seafood restaurant in an elegant harbourside villa on the Lido, reached by the seafront promenade between Opatija and Volosko.

🖂 Zert 8

☎ 051 712772

⌚ Daily 12–11; closed mid-Jun–mid-Jul

Ika (££)

With tables on the terrace beside an attractive pebble beach, this restaurant makes a good lunchtime stop on the Lungomare coast walk from Opatija to Lovran.

🖂 Ulica Maršala Tita 16, Ika

☎ 051 291777

⌚ Lunch and dinner daily

Le Mandrac (£££)

Chic harbourside restaurant in the fishing village of Volosko, offering fine food and wine in an elegant setting with an al fresco terrace in summer.

🖂 Frana Supila 10, Volosko

☎ 051 701357

⌚ Lunch and dinner daily

Mali Raj (£££)

This clifftop restaurant is situated on the Lungomare promenade, just outside Opatija on the path to Lovran. Fresh fish, fine linen and dreamy views over the bay.

🖾 Šetalište Maršala Tita 191
☎ 051 704074
🕓 Daily 10am–midnight

Poreč

Nono (£)

This place is reputed to serve some of the best and biggest pizzas in Croatia, baked in a brick oven. Also steaks, seafood, pasta and excellent salads.

🖾 Zagrebačka 4
☎ 052 453088
🕓 Daily 12–12

Peterokutna Kula (££)

Set in a restored 15th-century Venetian tower at the entrance to the old town, this funky restaurant offers a wide-ranging menu of fish and grilled meats.

🖾 Decumanus 1
☎ 052 451378
🕓 Daily 12–12

Sofora (££)

Fresh fish and seafood in a stunning seafront location, right on the promenade beside the jetty, so you can sit and watch the boats come and go to the island of Sveti Nikola.

🖾 Obala Maršala Tita 13
☎ 052 432053
🕓 Daily 12–10

Pula

Valsabbion (£££)

Smart, exclusive restaurant in a boutique hotel overlooking the marina, with a choice of six-course tasting menus and a mammoth 11-course gastronomic menu based on fresh, seasonal 'slow food'.

🖾 Pješčana Uvala
☎ 052 218033
🕓 Daily 12–12

Vela Nera (£££)

Fresh fish and lobster at one of the top restaurants in Istria. The house speciality is a risotto of shrimps, peaches and sparkling wine.

🖾 Pješčana Uvala
☎ 052 219209
🕓 Daily 12–12

Rovinj

La Puntuleina (£££)

Fashionable wine bar and restaurant in a romantic setting, perched above the rocks with a balcony over the sea. Creative Istrian cuisine based on truffles and fresh fish.

🖾 Ulica Svetog Križa 38
☎ 052 813186
🕓 Thu–Tue 12–12

Veli Jože (££)

Rustic *konoba* by the harbour steps offering first-class Istrian cuisine at wooden tables both inside and out. Specialities include steak with truffles.

🖾 Ulica Svetog Križa 3
☎ 052 816337
🕓 Daily 11am–midnight, Apr–Dec

Vodnjan

Vodnjanka (££)

Chef Svjetlana uses the freshest seasonal produce, such as Istrian ham, cheese, asparagus, mushrooms and snails, at this cosy family-run restaurant.

🖾 Istarska
☎ 052 511435
🕓 Mon–Sat 11–11, also Sun 6pm–midnight in summer

Vrsar and Limski Kanal

Fjord (££)

Busy restaurant with a large open-air terrace overlooking the jetty where the tour boats stop. The menu features fresh fish and seafood from the fjord.

🖾 Sveti Lovreč
☎ 052 448222
🕓 Daily 12–11

Vegetarians

Vegetarianism is not really understood in Croatia, and even dishes such as *grah* (bean soup) and meneštra (mixed vegetables) often contain pieces of meat. Note too that many so-called vegetarian dishes are prepared with meat stock. Croatia produces a wealth of organic vegetables but these rarely appear on restaurant menus. Unless you eat fish, you will probably have to stick to pasta, omelettes and salads. One popular side dish is *blitva*, which is similar to spinach and is usually served fried with potatoes and olive oil.

Dubrovnik

Fish and seafood

Fresh fish and seafood appear all along the Adriatic coast. Common varieties of white fish include John Dory, bass, bream and sole, while seafood could be mussels, oysters, scampi or prawns. Fish is usually served grilled and sold by weight—allow up to 500g (1lb) per person. A popular dish in Dalmatia is *brodet*, which consists of mixed fish casseroled with garlic, tomato and herbs and served on a bed of polenta.

Antunini (££)

With its plush red curtains, gilded mirrors and chandeliers, this restaurant recreates the feel of Ragusa's medieval guilds. Good lobster salad and fish stew.

- ✉ Prijeko 30
- ☎ 020 321199
- ⏲ Daily 9am–midnight

Buffet Škola (£)

The thick crusty sandwiches here are the best in town, stuffed full of Dalmatian cheese and ham. Found on an alley off the Stradun, with steps leading up to Prijeko.

- ✉ Antuninska 1
- ☎ 020 321096
- ⏲ Daily 8am–3am

Café Festival (£)

Destroyed by shells in 1991, this popular café is open again and is the best place for people-watching on the Stradun. Good coffee, cakes and Italian bruschetta.

- ✉ Stradun 1
- ☎ 020 321148
- ⏲ Daily 9am–midnight

Kamenice (££)

The name means 'oyster' and this busy lunchtime bar on the market square serves a simple but delicious menu of seafood, fried fish, risotto and salads.

- ✉ Poljana Gundulićeva 8
- ☎ 020 323682
- ⏲ Daily 7am–10pm

Lokanda Peskarija (££)

Popular open-air fish restaurant right by the Old Port, serving mussels, prawns, squid, grilled fish and seafood risotto to a mixed crowd of locals and tourists.

- ✉ Na Ponti

☎ 020 324750
⏲ Daily 8am–midnight

Mea Culpa (£)

Bustling pizzeria in the back lanes of the old town, with tables out of doors on a cobbled street. Pizzas, pasta dishes and salads.

- ✉ Za Rokom 3
- ☎ 020 424819
- ⏲ Daily 8am–midnight

Nautika (£££)

Top-notch fish and seafood in the old nautical academy outside Pile Gate, with two floors of dining plus a seafront summer terrace.

- ✉ Brsalje 3
- ☎ 020 442526
- ⏲ Daily 12–12

Orhan (£££)

Charming and romantic fish restaurant overlooking a small cove beach beneath Fort Lovrijenac. On summer evenings, you dine on a seaside terrace.

- ✉ Od Tabakarije 1
- ☎ 020 414183
- ⏲ Daily 11am–midnight

Rozarij (££)

On a busy street of tourist restaurants, this one stands out for its cosy atmosphere and authentic Dalmatian cuisine, such as black cuttlefish risotto.

- ✉ Zlatarska 4
- ☎ 020 321257
- ⏲ Daily 11am–midnight

Sesame (££)

Choose from pasta, salads, vegetarian dishes and ham and cheese plates at this arty bistro, a short walk from the old town outside Pile Gate.

- ✉ Ulica Dante Alighierija
- ☎ 020 412190
- ⏲ Daily 8am–11pm

Dalmatia

Brač

Konoba Marija (££)

A 4km (2-mile) clifftop path from Zlatni Rat beach leads to this stunningly situated *konoba*, with meat and fish cooked on an open grill on a shady terrace high above the sea.

🖂 Murvica, Bol
☎ 091 524 7439
🕒 Daily 10am–midnight, Apr–Oct

Palute (££)

Harbourside restaurant offering grilled meat and fish dishes on a seafront terrace, beside the port where the ferries arrive from Split.

🖂 Porat 4, Supetar
☎ 021 631730
🕒 Daily 10am–midnight, Apr–Oct

Vidova Gora (££)

This small *konoba* on the summit of Vidova Gora is open in summer, offering a simple menu of ham, cheese and roast lamb, accompanied by local wine and stunning views.

🖂 Vidova Gora
☎ 021 549061
🕒 Daily 10am–midnight, Apr–Oct

Cavtat

Galija (£££)

Situated at the end of the seafront promenade, this traditional wine cellar has a lovely summer terrace serving creative fish dishes, risottos and grills.

🖂 Vuličevićeva 1
☎ 020 478566
🕒 Daily 11am–midnight, Mar–Oct

Hvar

Bounty (££)

Simple menu of grilled meats, pasta, salad and seafood in a perfect setting beside the inner harbour. Grilled fish and seafood risotto are popular choices.

🖂 Mandrac, Hvar town
☎ 021 742565
🕒 Daily 11am–midnight, Apr–Oct

Konoba Dominko (£££)

This rustic tavern, set just back from the harbour in Jelsa, specializes in lamb, pork or octopus baked under a metal bell—must be ordered 24 hours in advance.

🖂 Jelsa
☎ 021 761441
🕒 Dinner only in summer

Konoba Menego (££)

Simple local produce, such as goat's cheese with honey or figs in brandy, in an old stone house on the castle steps. The owners make their own wines.

🖂 Groda, Hvar town
☎ 021 742036
🕒 Daily 12–2, 5–10, Apr–Oct

Luna (££)

Fashionable, offbeat bistro and roof garden with Italian-influenced cuisine, such as fresh pasta, steak with truffles and fish casserole.

🖂 Ulica Petra Hektorovića 5, Hvar town
☎ 021 741400
🕒 Daily 12–12, Apr–Dec

Paladini (£££)

Fresh fish and authentic Dalmatian cuisine served in a 16th-century palace overlooking the main square, or in a garden of orange and lemon trees in summer.

🖂 Ulica Petra Hektorovića 4, Hvar town
☎ 021 742104
🕒 Daily 12–3, 6–12, May–Dec

Wine

House wine is invariably priced by the litre, and can be ordered in 50cl or 25cl jugs or by the glass. Although it lacks sophistication, it is generally of good quality and reasonably priced. More expensive wines (► 69) are sold by the bottle. Wine is produced on the Pelješac Peninsula and on all the Dalmatian islands, particularly Brač, Hvar, Korčula and Vis.

Picnic food

A popular choice in summer is to take a picnic to a remote island or beach. Markets in all the main towns open early and sell fresh bread, cheese, ham, salami, salad and fruit. Bakeries (*pekarnica*) can be found almost everywhere, selling bread and *burek* (filo pastry filled with meat or cheese). Some of them will also make up sandwiches for you to take away.

Tony (££)

Down-to-earth harbourside bar where fishermen come for breakfast after a morning's catch—just the place for a snack while waiting for your ferry.

- ✉ Sućuraj
- ☎ No phone
- ⏰ Daily 6am–midnight

Zlatna Školjka (£££)

Chic restaurant specializing in 'slow food', with creative variations on local dishes such as gnocchi with almonds and rabbit with figs.

- ✉ Ulica Petra Hektorovića 8, Hvar town
- ☎ 098 168 8797
- ⏰ Daily 12–3, 7–12, Apr–Oct

Korčula

Adio Mare (££)

Bustling *konoba* in the old town, with communal wooden benches and fishing nets on the walls. Classic Dalmatian cuisine. No reservations.

- ✉ Ulica Svetog Roka 2, Korčula town
- ☎ 020 711253
- ⏰ Daily 6pm–midnight, May–Oct

Maslina (£)

Family-run restaurant on the road from Korčula to Lumbarda. The speciality is *pogača*, like Italian *foccacia* bread topped with cheese, olives and vegetables.

- ✉ Lumbarajska Cesta
- ☎ 020 711720
- ⏰ Daily 11am–midnight in summer, 5pm–midnight in winter

Morski Konjic (££)

Romantic setting on the sea walls, with tables just above the water. Fresh fish is expensive but there are simpler choices such as salads and grilled meat.

- ✉ Šetalište Petra Kanavelića, Korčula town
- ☎ 020 711878
- ⏰ Daily 8am–1am, Apr–Oct

Nacionalni Park Krka

Kristijan (£)

In an old stone mill above the jetty at Roški Slap, this serves simple plates of cured ham and cheese with bread, olives and wine.

- ✉ Roški Slap
- ☎ No phone
- ⏰ Lunch daily, Apr–Oct

Mljet

Mali Raj (££)

The name means 'little paradise' and the setting on the shores of Veliko Jezero lake is heavenly. Typical Dalmatian cuisine, including grilled meat and fish.

- ✉ Babine Kuće
- ☎ 020 744115
- ⏰ Daily 10am–midnight, May–Sep

Murter

Konoba Karaka (££)

First-class grilled meat and fish in an alley beside the port, where boats leave for the Kornati islands. Platters of grilled fish to share.

- ✉ Ulica Matije Gupca
- ☎ 022 436006
- ⏰ Daily 12–12, Feb–Nov

Mate (£££)

This busy fish restaurant is based around a courtyard north from the harbour. Specialities are grilled fish and *brodet* (fish stew).

- ✉ Ulica Luke
- ☎ 022 435351
- ⏰ Daily 11–11, Apr–Sep

Tic-Tac (££)

Buzzy, fashionable bistro in a quiet street near the harbour, with the usual fresh fish dishes but also grilled vegetables and octopus sushi.

- ✉ Ulica Hrokošina 5
- ☎ 022 435230
- ⏰ Daily 12–12, Apr–Sep

Pelješac

Kapetanova Kuća (£££)

Mali Ston is famous for its oysters and this is the best

place to try them. Also mussels, lobster and fish.

✉ **Mali Ston**
☎ **020 754555**
◉ **Daily 9am–midnight**

Split
Hvaranin (£)
Modest *konoba* in the Varoš district, just back from the Riva, offering Dalmatian and Hvar island classics such as stuffed peppers, fried anchovies and boiled lamb.

✉ **Ulica Ban Mladenova 9**
☎ **091 547 7946**
◉ **Daily 11am–midnight**

Kod Joze (££)
Traditional wine-cellar serving fresh fish, steaks, risottos and grilled vegetables in an old stone house or on the terrace, in a quiet lane outside the centre.

✉ **Sredmanuška 4**
☎ **021 347397**
◉ **Daily 9am–midnight**

Varoš (£££)
This tavern in the Varoš district has fishing nets on the walls and serves fresh fish as well as veal, lamb and octopus cooked under the *peka* (metal lid).

✉ **Ulica Ban Mladenova 7**
☎ **021 396138**
◉ **Daily 9am–midnight**

Trogir
Fontana (££)
Terrace restaurant on the Riva with a good range of meat and seafood dishes from *ćevapčići* to grilled fish and Dalmatian stews.

✉ **Obrov 1**
☎ **021 884811**
◉ **Daily 12–11**

Mirkec (£)
Occupying a prime position on the waterfront, this pizzeria makes a good lunchtime spot, with salads, pasta dishes and pizzas.

✉ **Budislavićeva 15**
☎ **021 883042**
◉ **Daily 10am–midnight**

Vis
Bako (££)
Small fish restaurant right by the water's edge, offering anchovies, sardines, lobster and fresh fish on a vine-covered terrace.

✉ **Gundulićeva 1, Komiža**
☎ **021 713742**
◉ **Daily 6pm–midnight in summer**

Doručak Kod Tihane (£££)
Seafood risotto, grilled squid, mussels and fresh fish are all on the menu at this romantic harbourside restaurant, whose name means 'Breakfast at Tiffany's'.

✉ **Obala Sveti Jurja 5, Vis town**
☎ **021 718472**
◉ **Daily 6am–9pm (earlier and later in season)**

Jastožera (£££)
Chic sailors' hangout in Komiža's old lobster-pot house, with wooden platforms above the water and magical sea views. Expensive fish and lobster.

✉ **Gundulićeva 6, Komiža**
☎ **021 713407**
◉ **Daily 5pm–2am in summer**

Vatrica (££)
Traditional *konoba* in the village of Kut, specializing in barbecued fish and spaghetti with lobster. Wooden tables on the waterfront, a short walk from Vis town.

✉ **Obala Kralja Krešimira 15, Kut**
☎ **021 711574**
◉ **Daily 9am–2am in summer, 5–11pm in winter**

Villa Kaliopa (£££)
Fresh fish and seafood in the walled garden of the 16th-century Garibaldi Palace. Elegant, romantic, expensive, and popular with visiting yachtsmen on summer evenings.

✉ **Ulica Vladimira Nazora 32, Vis town**
☎ **021 711755**
◉ **Daily 12–3, 5–2 in summer**

Spirits
The Croatians like their strong drinks, and stallholders at local markets sell a weird and wonderful array of home-made spirits and liqueurs in brightly coloured bottles. After a meal, you may be offered a glass of *rakija* or *grappa* on the house. The most common kinds are *šljivovica* (plum brandy) and *travarica* (herb brandy), but there are also local variations based on pears, walnuts, juniper and mistletoe. *Živjeli* (cheers)!

99

Zagreb

Prices
Prices are approximate, based on a double room in summer, excluding tourist tax:

£ = under 500kn
££ = 500kn–1,000kn
£££ = over 1,000kn

You can usually get a single room for around 75 per cent of the cost of a double. Hotel prices vary considerably between seasons, especially on the coast, though many seaside hotels are closed in winter. The tourist tax varies according to the season and the class of hotel.

Arcotel Allegra (£££)
Billed as Zagreb's first design hotel, this offers 151 rooms with contemporary furnishings, DVD and internet connection. Close to bus and railway stations.
www.arcotel.at/allegra
✉ Branimirova 29
☎ 01 469 6000

Dubrovnik (£££)
Built in 1929 and recently restored, this is the most centrally located of the top-of-the-range hotels. Some of the rooms overlook the main square.
www.hotel-dubrovnik.htnet.hr
✉ Ulica Ljudevita Gaja 1
☎ 01 487 3555

Ilica (££)
This small, friendly hotel has just 12 rooms, on Zagreb's main shopping street a short walk from Trg Bana Jelačića. A good budget choice in the heart of the city.
www.hotel-ilica.hr
✉ Ilica 102
☎ 01 377 7522

Jägerhorn (££)
Small, simply furnished hotel set around a courtyard just off the main square. The restaurant here is famed for its game dishes.
www.hotel-pansion-jaegerhorn.hr
✉ Ilica 14
☎ 01 483 3877

Janica (£)
Alpine lodge near the summit of Medvednica, offering single, double and triple rooms with showers. Set in a meadow among the pinewoods above the city.
www.hunjka.hr
✉ Sljemenska Cesta
☎ 01 458 0397

Palace (£££)
The oldest hotel in Zagreb opened in 1907 and it is still full of old-world charm, with antique furniture, Viennese salons and views over a peaceful green park.
www.palace.hr
✉ Strossmayerova Trg 10
☎ 01 481 4611

Regent Esplanade (£££)
Traditionally the top address in town, this luxury hotel near the railway station reopened in 2004 and is once again the meeting-place of the rich and famous of Zagreb.
www.regenthotels.com
✉ Mihanovićeva 1
☎ 01 456 6666

Sliško (££)
Small, family-run hotel with simple but comfortable rooms in a quiet street close to the bus station, a 30-minute walk or short tram ride from the centre.
www.slisko.hr
✉ Ulica Bunićeva 7
☎ 01 618 4777

Vila Tina (££)
A good choice on the outskirts of the city, with just 16 tastefully decorated rooms and an indoor pool in a family-run hotel close to Maksimir Park.
www.vilatina.com
✉ Bukovačka Cesta 213
☎ 01 244 5138

Westin Zagreb (£££)
This high-rise hotel is firmly aimed at business travellers, with facilities including solarium, fitness centre and internet access.
www.westin.com/zagreb
✉ Kršnjavoga 1
☎ 01 489 2000

Inland Croatia

Kopački Rit
Galid (£)
Simple rooms in a bungalow attached to a family home in the village of Bilje, 4km (2 miles) from the entrance to the nature park. Includes home-made breakfast.
✉ Ritska 1, Bilje
☎ 031 750393

Lonjsko Polje
Ravlić (£)
Cosy farmhouse accommodation on the top floor of a wooden cottage with views over the river. Excellent home cooking but the bathroom is outdoors.
✉ Mužilovčica 72
☎ 044 710151

Osijek
Osijek (££)
This high-rise hotel was completely rebuilt in 2004, with modern facilities such as wireless internet access. Ask for a room overlooking the riverside promenade.
www.hotel-osijek.hr
✉ Šamačka 4
☎ 031 230333

Plitvička Jezera
Jezero (££)
The biggest and best of the three hotels inside the national park, with views, sauna and steam baths.
www.np-plitvicka-jezera.hr
✉ Plitvička Jezera
☎ 053 751400

Samobor
Livadić (£)
Charming family-run hotel on the main square; antiques, a Viennese-style salon and courtyard serving delicious coffee and cakes.
www.hotel-livadic.hr
✉ Trg Kralja Tomislava 1
☎ 01 336 5850

Varaždin
Maltar (£)
Modest hotel with 15 simply furnished rooms, a short walk from the town centre. Breakfast 6–noon.
✉ Ulica Prešernova 1
☎ 042 311100

Turist (£)
The biggest hotel in town has 100 rooms in a modern building just outside the centre.
www.hotel-turist.hr
✉ Aleja Kralja Zvonimira
☎ 042 395395

Vukovar
Lav (££)
Completely destroyed during the war, this hotel was rebuilt and reopened in 2005 as a symbol of Vukovar's resilience. Some rooms look out over the River Danube.
www.hotel-lav.hr
✉ Strossmayerova 18
☎ 032 445100

Zagorje
Dvorac Bežanec (£££)
Croatia's top country-house hotel is set in a 17th-century mansion near Pregrada, with antique furniture, fine food and wine and an atmosphere of unashamed luxury.
www.bezanec.hr
✉ Valentinovo, Pregrada
☎ 049 376800

Lojzekova Hiža (£)
One of the best examples of agrotourism in the region, with attic rooms in a wooden farmhouse offering home cooking and horse-riding in the meadows and woods.
www.lojzekovahiza.com
✉ Gusakovec 116 (signposted off the road from Marija Bistrica to Donja Stubica)
☎ 049 469325

Agrotourism
In areas such as the Zagorje, Lonjsko Polje and Plitvice Lakes, you will come across signs advertising *agroturizam* or *seoski turizam* on working farms. Accommodation varies from basic to luxurious, but all offer an insight into rural Croatia and a chance to connect with the rhythms of country life. Agrotourism is at its most developed in inland Istria—see www.istra.com/ agroturizam.

Istria
and Kvarner

Lighthouses

Eleven of Croatia's lighthouses have been converted into self-catering apartments, sleeping between two and eight people. Of these, three are on the mainland and the rest are on remote islands, making this a real away-from-it-all adventure. In Istria, there are lighthouses at Cape Savudrija near Umag and on the Lanterna Peninsula near Poreč, and on the islands of Sveti Ivan near Rovinj and Porer near Pula. You can find information on staying in lighthouses at www.adriatica.net.

Brijuni Islands
Neptun (££)

Enjoy Brijuni after the daytrippers have left by staying in this harbourside hotel. Bicycles, boats and horses available for hire.
www.np-brijuni.hr
⊠ Veli Brijun
☎ 052 525100

Motovun
Kaštel (££)

Stylish family-run hotel on the main square, with a shady garden and roof terrace giving views across the Mirna Valley. The restaurant specializes in truffle dishes.
www.hotel-kastel-motovun.hr
⊠ Trg Andrea Antico 7
☎ 052 681607

Opatija
Ika (£)

If you can't afford Opatija prices, stay in this small beach hotel, an hour's walk along the promenade. Some rooms have shutters opening to a view of the sea.
www.hotel-ika.hr
⊠ Ulica Maršala Tita 16, Ika
☎ 051 291777

Kvarner-Amalia (£££)

Opened in 1884, this grand Hapsburg-era hotel perfectly captures the faded elegance of *fin-de-siècle* Opatija, with its Crystal Ballroom and ornate classical façade.
www.liburnia.hr
⊠ Ulica Tomašića 1
☎ 051 271233

Millennium (£££)

Striking modern hotel set in a peach-coloured villa in the heart of town, with gardens leading down to the beach. Facilities include heated indoor and outdoor pools.

www.ugohoteli.hr
⊠ Šetalište Maršala Tita 109
☎ 051 202000

Mozart (£££)

This stylish boutique hotel sets out to recreate Opatija's golden age, with Viennese-style salons and staff in period costume. Most rooms have balconies.
www.hotel-mozart.hr
⊠ Šetalište Maršala Tita 138
☎ 051 718260

Villa Ariston (££)

Royalty and film stars have stayed at this elegant 19th-century villa, with beautiful flower gardens and stone terraces leading down to the seafront promenade.
www.villa-ariston.hr
⊠ Šetalište Maršala Tita 179
☎ 051 271379

Poreč
Fortuna (£££)

Large, modern hotel on the wooded island of Sveti Nikola, with views to the old town and shuttle boats from the harbour in summer.
www.riviera.hr
⊠ Otok Sveti Nikola
☎ 052 408200
⊙ Apr–Oct

Neptun (££)

One of the few hotels in Poreč to stay open all year, this has a central position on the seafront promenade. Some rooms have balconies.
www.riviera.hr
⊠ Obala Marđala Tita 15
☎ 052 400800

Pula
Rivijera (££)

This mustard-coloured relic from the Hapsburg era would not be out of place in Opatija or Zagreb. Not as

grand as it looks but a convenient, central location.
www.arenaturist.hr
🏠 Splitska 1
☎ 052 211166

Scaletta (££)
With 12 rooms in a townhouse beside the Roman arena, this stylish hotel makes a good choice in the centre of town.
🏠 Ulica Flavijevska 26
☎ 052 541025

Valsabbion (£££)
Luxury hotel with 10 rooms overlooking a marina and pebble beach, and a beauty centre with hydromassage pool. The restaurant (➤ 95) is one of the best in Croatia.
www.valsabbion.hr
🏠 Pješčana Uvala
☎ 052 218033

Rab
Ros Maris (£££)
Former harbourside hotel now a classy spa and wellness resort, with swimming pool, sauna and stylish restaurants and bars.
www.rosmaris.com
🏠 Obala Kralja Petra Krešimira
☎ 051 778899

Rovinj
Adriatic (££)
The oldest hotel in Rovinj occupies a prime position by the harbourside, with a café terrace and the best rooms having views out to sea.
www.adriaresorts.hr
🏠 Obala Pina Budicina
☎ 052 815088

Istra (£££)
Large, modern hotel on the island of Crveni Otok, with shuttle boats to Rovinj. Swimming pools, tennis courts and a pebble beach.
www.adriaresorts.hr
🏠 Otok Sv Andrije-S Andrea
☎ 052 802500
Ⓒ Apr–Oct

Katarina (£££)
German-owned hotel in an early 20th-century villa, surrounded by gardens on its own island with views of the old town.
www.hotelinsel-katarina.com
🏠 Otok Sveti Katarina
☎ 052 804100
Ⓒ Apr–Oct

Villa Angelo d'Oro (£££)
Charming hotel in a restored 17th-century bishop's palace in the back streets of the old town, with a peaceful garden, rooftop loggia and private yacht for hire.
www.rovinj.at
🏠 Via Svalba 38-42
☎ 052 840502

Villa Valdibora (£££)
Four fully serviced apartments in a 17th-century baroque mansion, combining antique style with modern comforts such as computer, microwave and satellite TV.
www.valdibora.com
🏠 Chiurco Silvano 8
☎ 052 845040

Vodnjan
Stancija Negričani (££)
Ten rooms in an old stone farmhouse with a swimming pool in the gardens and excellent home-cooked food. A peaceful retreat, in the countryside but not far from the coast.
www.stancijanegricani.com
🏠 Off the road from Vodnjan to Barban
☎ 052 391084

Vrsar and Limski Kanal
Agroturizam Matošević (££)
Simple accommodation on a working farm in the village of Kloštar, with views over the vineyards and huge farmhouse dinners accompanied by local wine.
www.matosevic.com
🏠 Kloštar 21
☎ 052 444492

Camping
Croatia has more than 150 official campsites. All are equipped with hot water, showers and toilets and many have restaurants and swimming pools. The biggest concentration is in Istria, though they are spread out all along the Adriatic coast. A number of campsites are exclusively reserved for naturists, including Koversada at Vrsar, Europe's largest naturist resort. A full list of campsites is available at www.camping.hr and www.croatia.hr; for information on naturism, check out www.cronatur.com.

Dalmatia

Boutique hotels

A recent trend has been the opening of small, individually designed hotels, many in converted townhouses and palaces in Croatia's historic towns. In architectural terms, these are a world away from the mass-market beach hotels erected during the Communist era. Among the best examples are the Pucić Palace in Dubrovnik (▶ below), Villa Angelo d'Oro in Rovinj (▶ 103) and Mozart in Opatija (▶ 102).

Dubrovnik

Grand Villa Argentina (£££)

Film stars Richard Burton and Elizabeth Taylor, and the Yugoslav leader Tito, have all stayed at this smart hotel, with clifftop villas and a private beach and views.

www.hoteli-argentina.hr

✉ Frana Supila 14

☎ 020 440555

Hilton Imperial (£££)

One of the oldest hotels in Dubrovnik was restored after the war and reopened in 2005. All the luxuries you would expect and a central setting near Pile Gate.

www.hilton.com

✉ Ulica Dr Ante Starčevića

☎ 020 320320

Lapad (£££)

Old-style hotel with swimming pool on the Lapad Peninsula, facing Gruž harbour. A short bus ride from the old city, with boat trips available to nearby beaches.

www.hotel-lapad.hr

✉ Lapadska Obala 37

☎ 020 432922

⏱ Apr–Nov

Pucić Palace (£££)

Luxury townhouse hotel in an 18th-century palace on the market square, with dark oak floors, antique furniture, modern art and a private yacht for guests.

www.thepucicpalace.com

✉ Ulica Od Puča 1

☎ 020 326200

Stari Grad (£££)

One of only two hotels within the medieval walls, this has eight rooms in an old townhouse close to Pile Gate. The rooftop terrace has views over the city.

www.hotelstarigrad.com

✉ Od Sigurate 4

☎ 020 322244

Sumartin (££)

Small, old–fashioned hotel in a garden of palm trees at the centre of the Lapad Peninsula, convenient for nearby beaches and for bus trips to the old town.

✉ Šetalište Kralja Zvonimira 31

☎ 020 436146

Villa Dubrovnik (£££)

Romantic seaside villa set among orange trees, with its own beach and shuttle boats to the old town. All rooms have balconies with views.

www.villa-dubrovnik.hr

✉ Ulica Vlaha Bukovca 6

☎ 020 422933

⏱ Mar–Nov

Brač

Kaštil (££)

With a perfect position right on the seafront, this small hotel has 32 rooms in a traditional stone building by the harbour. Zlatni Rat is a 2km (1 mile) stroll away.

www.kastil.hr

✉ Ulica Frane Radića 1, Bol

☎ 021 635995

⏱ Mar–Oct

Cavtat

Croatia (£££)

Huge, modern hotel on the Sustjepan Peninsula, with views across the town and a full range of facilities including swimming pools, tennis courts and beaches.

www.hoteli-croatia.hr

✉ Šetalište Sustjepan

☎ 020 475555

⏱ Feb–Nov

Supetar (££)

Owned by the same company as Hotel Croatia,

this old stone house by the harbour has simply furnished rooms and a prime location on the waterfront promenade.

www.hoteli-croatia.hr/supetar

✉ Obala A Star evi a 27

☎ 020 479833

◉ Apr–Oct

Hvar

Palace (£££)

The top hotel in Hvar is in the old Venetian governor's palace, with views across the harbour from the terrace. Facilities include a heated seawater pool.

www.suncanihvar.hr

✉ Trg Svetog Stjepana, Hvar town

☎ 021 741966

Slavija (££)

Good mid-priced choice in an old stone building on the harbourside, with breakfast served on a seafront terrace in view of the nearby yachts.

www.suncanihvar.hr

✉ Obala Oslobođenja, Hvar town

☎ 021 741820

Korčula

Korčula (££)

Old-fashioned hotel on the waterfront, near the entrance to the old town, with 20 comfortable rooms and a seaside terrace.

www.htp-korcula.hr

✉ Obala Vinka Paletina

☎ 020 711078

Murter

Marina Hramina (££)

You don't need a yacht to stay here as there are also a few rooms, decked out in nautical style with balconies overlooking the marina.

www.marina-hramina.hr

✉ Put Gradine

☎ 022 434411

Nacionalni Park Krka

Skradinski Buk (££)

Small, family-run hotel in the harbourside village of Skradin, near the entrance to the national park.

www.skradinskibuk.hr

✉ Burinovac, Skradin

☎ 022 771771

Nacionalni Park Mljet

Odisej (££)

The only hotel in the national park looks down over a small cove in Pomena. Walking, cycling and sailing are popular activities here.

www.hotelodisej.hr

✉ Pomena

☎ 020 744022

Split

Jadran (££)

Small, modern hotel situated in a pretty bay, a short walk from the centre. Excellent sports facilities including an Olympic-size pool, tennis courts, sauna and jacuzzi.

www.hoteljadran.hr

✉ Sustipanski Put 23

☎ 021 398622

Trogir

Concordia (££)

Rooms in an 18th-century townhouse on the Riva, with views across the marina from the seafront terrace.

www.concordia-hotel.htnet.hr

✉ Obala Bana Berislavića 22

☎ 021 885400

Pasike (££)

Small family-run hotel which opened in 2004, with seven rooms in an old townhouse decorated with 19th- and 20th-century furniture.

www.hotelpasike.com

✉ Sinjska

☎ 021 885185

Vis

Tamaris (£)

Many people arrive in Vis on their own yacht but if not, stay in this Hapsburg villa by the harbour, with views across the bay from its spacious, shuttered rooms.

✉ Obala Sveti Jurja 20, Vis town

☎ 021 711350

Private accommodation

The cheapest rooms on the islands and coast are usually to be found in private accommodation. Staying with Croatian families can also give a good insight into local life. At bus stations and ferry ports, expect to be met by women offering *sobe* (rooms) and *apartmani* (apartments); otherwise, visit one of the local agencies or simply look out for signs. The standard of accommodation varies and not all of it is registered so it is worth looking before you agree a price.

Zagreb

Love tokens

A speciality of Zagreb and the Zagorje is the *licitarsko srce*, an iced and decorated gingerbread heart flavoured with pepper and honey. Although they are edible, they are not designed to be eaten and are traditionally given as love tokens. You can buy them at shops all over the region, or at the tourist information centre in Trg Bana Jelačića in Zagreb.

Zagreb's main shopping street is Ilica, which runs west of Trg Bana Jelačića and is lined with shops selling the latest clothing and shoes. In the upper town, Radićeva and Tkalčićeva have a more offbeat, fashionable feel, with art galleries and trendy boutiques. Locals do much of their shopping in modern American-style malls, such as Importanne (beneath the railway station), Rotunda Centar (near Trg Bana Jelačića) and Centar Kaptol (near the cathedral).

Books
Algoritam
Large bookshop in the base of the Hotel Dubrovnik, with foreign-language books and magazines in the basement. Good selection of Croatian literature, history and politics.

✉ Ulica Ljudevita Gaja 1
☎ 01 481 8672

Department Stores
Nama
Historic state-owned department store on the corner of the main square, now a lively shopping centre with a range of clothing and food shops.

✉ Ilica 4
☎ 01 455 2233

Food & Drink
Dolac Market
The city's main market is located on a raised terrace above Trg Bana Jelačića. Farmers sell fresh fruit and vegetables at outdoor stalls, with meat, fish, bread and cheese sold from indoor halls. There is also a flower market on the edge of the square. An essential Zagreb experience even if you don't want to shop.

✉ Dolac
🕐 Mon–Fri 7–4, Sat–Sun 7–12

Galerija Pršut
The best range of cured hams from Istria and Dalmatia, plus salami, cheese, wines and olive oil.

✉ Vlaška 7
☎ 01 481 6129

Iločki Podrumi
On a street with several wine cellars, this one sells white wines from the Slavonian town of Ilok.

✉ Kaptol 12
☎ 01 481 4593

Superkonzum
Everything you could ever want at Zagreb's biggest supermarket. There is another branch inside the Importanne shopping centre, beneath the railway station.

✉ Avenija Vukovar 275
☎ 01 230 0242

Zigante Tartufi
All kinds of truffles and truffle-based products from Istria.

✉ Rotunda Centar, Jurišićeva 19
☎ 01 481 7794

Ties
Croata
Silk ties, scarves and accessories sold in the home of the tie (▶ 40). The main branch is in the Oktogon passage near Trg Bana Jelačića. There are other branches in Dubrovnik, Split, Rijeka, Osijek, Varaždin and at airports.

✉ Prolaz Oktogon, Ilica 5; also at Kaptol 13
☎ 01 481 2726

Around the Country

Specialities of Croatia include lace from the island of Pag, lavender from Hvar and Croata silk ties. Another popular souvenir is a miniature ceramic replica of a traditional Istrian or Dalmatian house. Artists sell their work in the street in summer, particularly in the Istrian towns of Poreč, Rovinj, Grožnjan and Labin. All the main towns and coastal resorts have summer markets selling a variety of souvenirs, arts and crafts.

Markets are renowned for the quality of their fresh produce. Most towns have farmers' markets, where farmers sell fruit, vegetables, cheese, herbs, home-made wine, spirits and liqueurs. The following is a list of some of Croatia's specialist food and drink outlets.

Inland Croatia

Samobor
Obitelj Filipec
The Filipec family produce *bermet*, a vermouth flavoured with carob and figs, and *muštarda*, a sweet, spicy grape mustard dating back to a recipe from 1808.
✉ Stražnička 1
☎ 01 336 4835

Vukovar
Iločki Podrumi
The border town of Ilok is known for its excellent white wines and production has resumed after the war. Good buys here are Graševina, Chardonnay, Bijeli Pinot and Traminac.
✉ Ulica Dr Franje Tuđmana 72
☎ 032 590003

Istria

Buzet
Zigante Tartufi
Local farmer Giancarlo Zigante discovered the world's biggest truffle in 1999 and he now owns a chain of shops selling truffle-based products and other Istrian specialities. Fresh truffles are available in autumn; at other times you can buy preserved truffles, truffle oil and truffle paste. There is also an excellent selection of Istrian wines. The main shop is in Buzet, but there are branches in Buje, Grožnjan, Livade, Novigrad, Pula, Umag, Zagreb and Munich.
✉ Trg Fontana
☎ 052 812154

Dalmatia

Dubrovnik
Dubrovačka Kuća
Small shop and art gallery near the Dominican monastery selling a wide range of Dalmatian and Croatian wines, *rakija* and liqueurs.
✉ Ulica Svetog Dominika
☎ 020 322092

Pelješac
Matuško Vina
At the heart of the Pelješac Peninsula, the village of Potomje is the centre of wine production and this small winery sells Dingač and Plavac Mali red wines at reasonable prices, plus *prošek* (a sweet apéritif or dessert wine) and liqueurs. The nearby Dingač winery is better-known but also more expensive.
✉ Potomje
☎ 020 742393

Fairs in Istria
Istria is a paradise for gourmets, producing first-class ham, cheese, olives, truffles and wine. Much of this is on display at the monthly agricultural fairs, former cattle markets which continue to attract big crowds with a mix of food and craft stalls, and folk dancing. They take place in the towns of inland Istria on the following days:

Vodnjan—first Saturday
Pazin—first Tuesday
Žminj—second Wednesday
Motovun—third Monday
Buzet—third Thursday
Višnjan—last Thursday

Attractions

Looking after kids

Small children are particularly vulnerable to the sun and need to be well protected. Apply a high-factor sunscreen regularly, especially after swimming, and keep their heads covered during the heat of the day. A pair of plastic sandals is useful for rocky beaches and as protection against jellyfish and sea-urchins. Children and non-swimmers should always wear life-jackets for sailing and other hazardous activities.

Family outings

Besides those attractions listed here, children will also enjoy many adult activities including:
The cable-car ride on Medvednica (▶ 38)
The waterfalls and boat trips at Plitvice Lakes (▶ 21) and Krka National Park (▶ 83)
Seeing storks in the Lonjsko Polje (▶ 47)
Exploring the Roman arena at Pula (▶ 22)

Although it has few attractions aimed specifically at children, Croatia is still a great country for travelling with kids. With over 1,000km (620 miles) of coastline and more than 1,000 islands, the Adriatic provides limitless opportunities for swimming and water-based fun. The only disadvantage for children is the lack of sandy beaches—most natural beaches are either pebbles or rocks, while others described as beaches turn out to be artificial concrete platforms which are perfect for sunbathing but useless for building sandcastles.

Most hotels and campsites have swimming pools for children, and many organize 'kids' clubs' in summer with activities from beach volleyball to disco parties. Many hotels also have excellent sports facilities, ranging from a leisurely round of mini-golf to tennis, badminton, basketball and handball courts. Bike hire is another good option. If you want to get out on the water, you can hire a pedal-boat at some of the more popular beaches, while older and more adventurous children can learn to canoe, windsurf or sail a yacht. Children always seem to enjoy boat trips, whether it is a 'pirate cruise' on the Limski Kanal or taking the ferry to one of the Adriatic islands.

Zagreb
Prirodoslovni Muzej (Natural History Museum)
Old-fashioned but engaging museum in the upper town of Zagreb, with hundreds of stuffed animals and birds and a complete 8m (9-yard) long basking shark.
🖂 Ulica Demetrova 1
☎ 01 485 1700
🕒 Tue–Fri 10–5, Sat–Sun 10–1

Zoo
Brown bears, wolves, elephants, tigers, lions, leopards, crocodiles, chimpanzees, a penguin pool, an aquarium and a reptile house make this a popular day out. Children will also enjoy strolling in Maksimir Park, with its playgrounds and swings.
🖂 Maksimirski Perivoj
☎ 01 230 2199
🕒 Daily 9–8 in summer, 9–5 in winter (ticket office closes one hour before)

Inland Croatia
Osijek Zoo
Osijek's zoo was gutted during the recent war and many of the animals were moved, but it is open once again in a pleasant setting beside the River Drava.
🖂 2km (1 mile) from town centre
☎ 031 285234
🕒 Daily 8–8 in summer, 9–4 in winter

Staro Selo
The ethnographic museum village at Kumrovec (▶ 45) is always a hit with children, especially in summer when there are displays of craftmaking.
🖂 Kumrovec, Zagorje
☎ 049 500476
🕒 Daily 9–7, Apr–Oct; 9–4, Nov–Mar

Trakošćan
As well as exploring the castle (▶ 50), children can

enjoy taking a pedal-boat out for a trip on the lake in summer.
- ✉ **Trakošćan**
- ☎ **042 796422**
- 🕒 **Daily 9–6 in summer, 9–3 in winter**

Istria
Aquarium Poreč
Small aquarium in the heart of the old town, with colourful displays of Adriatic fish and a souvenir shop for the kids.
- ✉ **Ulica Glavinića 4, Poreč**
- ☎ **052 428720**
- 🕒 **Daily 9–9, Apr–Oct; 10–5, Nov–Mar**

Aquarium Pula
Situated in an old Hapsburg fortress on the Punta Verudela Peninsula, this aquarium features large seawater tanks filled with Adriatic fish and marine creatures.
- ✉ **Fort Verudela, Pula**
- ☎ **052 381402**
- 🕒 **Daily 9–9, Apr–Oct; Sat–Sun 11–5, Nov–Mar**

Aquarium Rovinj
One of Europe's oldest aquariums, founded in 1891, with enjoyable displays of starfish, puffer fish, lobsters and sea creatures.
- ✉ **Obala Giordano Paliage 5, Rovinj**
- ☎ **052 804712**
- 🕒 **Daily 9–9, Easter–Oct**

Brijuni Islands
Children will enjoy a miniature train ride through the safari park, which contains descendants of the animals presented to the Yugoslav leader Tito by visiting statesmen (► 57).
- ✉ **Boat trips from Fažana**
- ☎ **052 521880**

Mini Croatia
Opened in 2003, this miniature theme park features reproductions of famous buildings from across Croatia.
- ✉ **2km (1 mile) from centre of Rovinj on the road to Pazin**
- ☎ **091 206 8885**
- 🕒 **Daily 10–6, Apr–Oct**

Dalmatia
Bunari—Secrets of Šibenik
Šibenik is the unlikely destination for this multimedia experience, in the vaults of the 15th-century wells opposite the cathedral. Using techniques imported from theme parks, visitors can explore the city's heritage through interactive displays on themes ranging from shipwrecks to food and drink.
- ✉ **Trg Republike Hrvatske, Šibenik**
- ☎ **098 341175**
- 🕒 **Daily 8am–11pm**

Dubrovnik Aquarium
Housed in the ground floor of St John's Fort and built into the city walls, this excellent aquarium has seawater tanks containing coral, shells, starfish, seahorses, a loggerhead turtle and several varieties of Adriatic grouper.
- ✉ **Tvrđa Sveti Ivana, Dubrovnik**
- ☎ **020 323978**
- 🕒 **Daily 9–8 in summer, Mon–Sat 10–1 in winter**

Split Zoo
Small zoo at the summit of Marjan Hill, with bears, wolves and tigers as well as farm animals.
- ✉ **Kolombatićevo Šetalište 2**
- ☎ **021 394525**
- 🕒 **Daily 8–6**

Zoos
Whatever your views about keeping animals in captivity, you should be aware that animal welfare campaigners have criticized conditions in Croatia's zoos, with particular concern for Sony and Lanka, the elephants on the Brijuni Islands. In 2002, the Croatian government responded to pressure by rejecting a gift of two elephants from Sri Lanka to Osijek Zoo to replace one that had been moved during the war.

Classical Music and Drama

Croatian National Theatre

In Zagreb, the Croatian National Theatre is housed in a grandiose central European opera house, opened by the Hapsburg emperor Franz Josef I on a state visit to Zagreb in 1895. With its baroque furnishings, painted ceilings, ceremonial curtains and plush red seats, a visit here is a special experience whatever the performance. The theatre is home to the National Ballet and National Opera, but also hosts visiting companies throughout the year. There is another branch of the Croatian National Theatre at Split (☎ 021 344999)

Croatia has a rich cultural tradition. To find out what's on, ask at local tourist offices. In Zagreb, pick up a copy of the monthly *Events and Performances* or the free magazine *Zagreb In Your Pocket* from tourist offices and hotels.

Zagreb

Hrvatski Glazbeni Zavod (Croatian Music Institute)
Chamber and classical music.
✉ Gundulićeva 6
☎ 01 483 0822

Kazalište Komedija
Small theatre focusing on musicals and operettas.
✉ Kaptol 9
☎ 01 481 3200

Koncertna Dvorana Vatroslav Lisinski
Home to the Zagreb Philharmonic Orchestra.
✉ Trg Stjepana Radića 4
☎ 01 612 1166

Inland Croatia

Osijek
Hrvatsko Narodno Kazalište
Restored Hapsburg-era theatre.
✉ Županijska 9
☎ 031 220700

Varaždin
Hrvatsko Narodno Kazalište
Opened in 1873 and still staging some of the best Croatian drama.
✉ Ulica Augusta Cesarca 1
☎ 042 214688

Istria and Kvarner

Pula
Istarsko Narodno Kazalište
Home to the Pula Municipal Theatre and the Istrian National Theatre.
✉ Laginjina 5
☎ 052 212677

Rijeka
Hrvatsko Narodno Kazalište
Home to the Rijeka Symphony Orchestra.
✉ Uljarska 1
☎ 051 355900

Dalmatia

Dubrovnik
Dubrovački Simfonijski Orkestar (Dubrovnik Symphony Orchestra)
Performances in a Renaissance villa near Pile Gate, and in the Rector's Palace in summer.
✉ Ulica Dr Ante Starčevića 29
☎ 020 417110

Kazalište Marin Držica
Croatian drama in a theatre devoted to Ragusan playwright Marin Držić (1508–67).
✉ Pred Dvorom 3
☎ 020 321088

Hvar
Hvarsko Kazalište
One of the oldest community theatres in Europe, opened in 1612 and beautifully restored. Performances are staged throughout the summer season.
✉ Trg Svetog Stjepana
☎ 021 741059

Zadar
Hrvatska Kazališna Kuđa (Croatian Playhouse)
Zadar's top venue for a wide spectrum of music and drama.
✉ Široka Ulica 8
☎ 023 314586

Summer Festivals

In summer, concerts take place in churches, courtyards and open-air venues across the country. Below are some of the major events. Details from local tourist offices and on the festival websites.

Zagreb
International Folklore Festival
Held in late July, with daily performances of music and dance in the upper town and Trg Bana Jelačića.
www.msf.hr
☎ 01 450 1194

Inland Croatia

Osijek
Tamburica Festival
In eastern Slavonia the *kolo* (circle dance) is performed to the sound of the *tamburica*, a Balkan stringed instrument similar to a mandolin. A festival of *tamburica* music is held in Osijek in late May.
☎ 031 283253

Slavonski Brod
Brodsko Kolo
Croatia's oldest and most traditional festival of folk dance in mid-June.
☎ 035 445765

Varaždin
Varaždin Baroque Evenings
Classical concerts in the city's churches, palaces and theatre in late September and early October.
www.vbv.hr
☎ 042 212907

Istria

Grožnjan
Jeunesses Musicales Croatia
International summer school of young musicians with concerts in July and August.
www.hgm.hr
☎ 01 611 1604

Pula
Histria Festival
Opera, ballet, orchestral and pop concerts in the Roman arena in July and August.
www.histriafestival.com
☎ 052 522720

Istra Etno-Jazz
Modern jazz and world music in the Roman theatre and Svetvinčenat castle in July.
www.istraetnojazz.com
☎ 052 505620

Dalmatia

Dubrovnik
Summer Festival
The Libertas summer festival (10 July–25 August) is Croatia's biggest cultural event, with six weeks of open-air music and drama at venues including Fort Lovrijenac and the atrium of the Rector's Palace.
www.dubrovnik-festival.hr
☎ 020 326100

Split
Summer Festival
Opera, music and dance throughout the city from mid-July to mid-August, with some performances in the Peristyle courtyard of Diocletian's Palace.
www.hnk-split.hr
☎ 021 344999

Zadar
St Donat's Musical Evenings
Early music recitals in St Donat's Church in July and August.
www.kuz.hr
☎ 023 300430

The *moreška*
This ritualized sword dance has been performed on the island of Korčula since the 16th century. The story is a predictable tale of good overcoming evil, acted out by a Black and White King and their armies of followers as they fight over a beautiful Moorish maiden. The dance is performed in Korčula on Monday and Thursday evenings in summer, and across the island during the Festival of Sword Dances in July and August.

Bars and Nightlife

A Eurovision troubadour

Marko Breskovic, the owner of the Troubadour Jazz Café in Dubrovnik, was a member of the Dubrovački Trubaduri, a Sixties beat group who represented Yugoslavia in the 1968 Eurovision song contest at the Royal Albert Hall in London, finishing seventh with their song *Jedan Dan* (One Day). Marko can occasionally be seen on summer evenings joining in with impromptu jazz sessions on his double–bass.

Rather than sophisticated nightlife and clubbing, most people prefer to spend summer evenings sitting outside a bar with friends.

Zagreb

The liveliest streets are Tkalčićeva in the upper town, and Bogovićeva, just off Trg Bana Jelačića. Tkalčićeva is more youthful, fashionable and edgy, while Bogovićeva and the surrounding streets and squares are lined with busy open-air cafés and ice-cream parlours attracting a wide range of ages and nationalities.

Aquarius

The top venue for serious clubbers began as a wooden shack on the shores of Lake Jarun, 4km (2 miles) south of the city centre. Techno and dance music, with rock concerts on a summer terrace.
- ✉ Matije Ljubeka
- ☎ 01 364 0231
- ⓘ Tue–Sun 8pm–4am

BP Club

Popular basement jazz club near Trg Bana Jelačića.
- ✉ Ulica Nikole Tesle 7
- ☎ 01 481 4444
- ⓘ Daily 5pm–1am

Sax

Live music most nights, with an emphasis on jazz and blues.
- ✉ Palmotićeva 22
- ☎ 01 487 2836
- ⓘ Daily 9am–4am

Istria

Rovinj
Valentino

Cool cocktail bar where you sit on silk cushions on the rocks, watching the sunset and listening to mellow music with your feet almost dangling in the sea.
- ✉ Ulica Svetog Križa 28
- ☎ 052 830683
- ⓘ Daily 6pm–3am in summer

Dalmatia

Dubrovnik
Buža

Dubrovnik's most atmospheric bar, in a spectacular position on a palm-shaded waterfront terrace, perched on the rocks outside the city walls. Get there by following the sign saying 'Cold Drinks' through a gap in the walls and down the steps.
- ✉ Access from Ulica Od Margarite

Troubadour

Jazz café near the cathedral, with live music on an outdoor terrace at 10pm nightly in summer (see panel).
- ✉ Bunićeva Poljana 2
- ☎ 020 323476

Brač
Faces

Huge open-air disco on the hill above Bol, with dancing for 2,000 people every night in summer.
- ✉ Bol
- ☎ 021 635410

Hvar
Carpe Diem

Groovy seafront cocktail bar where the beautiful people meet in summer for jazz and Latin nights, full moon and 'après-beach' parties.
- ✉ Obala Oslobođenja, Hvar town
- ☎ 021 742369
- ⓘ Daily 9am–3am in summer

Spectator Sport

Basketball

The Croatians are passionate about basketball (*košarka*). Their most famous player was Dražen Petrović (1964–93), who represented Portland and New Jersey in the American NBA and led Croatia to an Olympic silver medal in 1992 shortly before his death in a car accident. His former club, Cibona, plays at the Dražen Petrović Centre in Zagreb. The other top teams are Split and Zadar. Matches take place on Saturday evenings between September and April.

Zagreb
Cibona
✉ Savska Cesta 30
☎ 01 484 3333

Dalmatia

Split
Košarkaški Klub Split
✉ Ulica Slobode 16
☎ 021 323650

Zadar
Košarkaški Klub Zadar
✉ Obala Kralja Tomislava 1
☎ 023 212441

Football

Football (*nogomet*) is a national obsession, which reached fever pitch in 1998 when Croatia finished third in the World Cup. The domestic league is dominated by the rivalry between the 'Blues' of Dinamo Zagreb and the 'Whites' of Hajduk Split. Dinamo were Croatian champions seven times between 1993 and 2003, including five consecutive years from 1996 to 2000, but have recently been eclipsed by Hajduk Split. Other first division clubs include NK Zagreb, and teams from Osijek, Pula, Rijeka, Varaždin and Zadar. The season begins in late July and continues to early December, resuming in late February after a winter break. In April and May, the top six teams form a mini-league to compete for the championship, while the bottom six face relegation play-offs. Matches take place at weekends, and it is generally easy to buy tickets on the gate. The Croatian national team play their games at Dinamo's Maksimir Stadium, which seats 40,000 spectators.

Zagreb
Dinamo Zagreb
✉ Maksimirska 128
☎ 01 232 3234

NK Zagreb
✉ Kranjčevićeva 4
☎ 01 366 8111

Dalmatia

Split
Hajduk Split
✉ Poljud Stadium, Mediteranskih Igara 2
☎ 021 539292

Tennis

The achievements of players such as Goran Ivanišević (► 14), Mario Ančić, Ivan Ljubičić and Iva Majoli have raised the profile of Croatian tennis. The biggest events are the ATP Challenger Series Zagreb Open, held in May at the Mladost sports park near Lake Jarun, and the Croatia Open, an ATP tour event, in the Istrian resort of Umag in July.

Handball (*rukomet*)

Croatia has enjoyed spectacular success in handball. The Yugoslav team won the first ever Olympic handball competition in Munich in 1972 and repeated the feat in Los Angeles in 1984. Since independence, Croatia has won Olympic gold medals in 1996 and 2004 as well as the world championships in 2003. The top domestic team is RK Zagreb.

Outdoor Activities

Scuba diving
The crystal-clear waters of the Adriatic are perfect for scuba diving and you will find diving schools all along the coast. All divers must have a certificate, which costs 100kn and is only available to those with a recognized qualification. Diving is forbidden within the Brijuni and Krka national parks, and only allowed in the Kornati Islands and Mljet when part of an organized group.

Look out for
Highly populated areas and major routes are now clear of mines and are safe to visit. However, in some isolated areas in the mountains and countryside land mines may still be a danger. You should therefore be careful not to stray from roads and paved areas without an experienced guide.

The mountains, lakes, rivers, islands and coast provide endless opportunities for enjoying the great outdoors.

Canoeing, kayaking and rafting
Local agencies in the main towns and resorts offer numerous adventures on Croatia's rivers in spring and summer. Canoeing and kayaking take place on the Dobra and Kupa rivers near Karlovac, the River Zrmanja near Zadar and the River Krka near Šibenik. Top destinations for white-water rafting include the Cetina Gorge at Omiš near Split, the River Korana downstream from the Plitvice Lakes, and the River Una, which forms the border between Croatia and Bosnia in northern Dalmatia. Canoeing, kayaking and rafting are potentially hazardous activities and you should make sure that full safety equipment is provided.

Golf
Golf has been slow to take off in Croatia but there are now plans for major development, with 22 courses under construction in Istria alone.

Zagreb
Golf & Country Club Zagreb
Short nine-hole course (par 30) which opened in 2004 near Lake Jarun. There are plans to build a championship course here.
✉ **Jadranska Avenija 6**
☎ **01 788 0481**

Inland Croatia
Dolina Kardinala
Eighteen-hole course and

golf academy which opened in 1998 between Karlovac and Samobor.
✉ **Krašić**
☎ **047 731100**

Istria
Brijuni Islands
Nine-hole course which opened in 1922 on the island of Veli Brijun, set among parkland with unusual sandy greens.
✉ **Veli Brijun**
☎ **052525882**

Golf Resort Motovun
Luxury German-owned 36-hole golf resort, scheduled for completion in 2005.
✉ **Motovun**
☎ **052 725100**

Hiking and climbing
There is gentle walking on the Adriatic islands, in the Medvednica mountain range near Zagreb and the Žumberak Hills near Samobor. For more challenging hikes, head for the Risnjak National Park or the Biokovo and Velebit massifs on the Dalmatian coast. There is good rock-climbing in the Paklenica and North Velebit national parks, and at Zlatni Rat forest park in Rovinj.

Skiing
Croatia is not a major winter sports destination, but there are three small-scale ski resorts with marked pistes, cable-cars and lifts, where skis and boots can be hired in winter. One is at Sljeme, on the summit of Medvednica (▶ 38); the others are at Bjelolasica and Platak, in the Gorski Kotar Mountains near Rijeka.

Sailing

There can be no better way of experiencing the Croatian islands and coast than from the deck of your own boat. The best months for sailing are May, June, September and October, though July and August are more suitable for beginners, with calm waters and a light *maestral* wind making for pleasant conditions. In winter, you need to look out for the *bora*, a strong northeasterly wind which can cause havoc for sailors, particularly in Kvarner bay where it can reach gale force for several days at a time.

Yachts and motorboats can be hired from most marinas, either bareboat (for which you must be an experienced sailor) or skippered. The website www.croatia.hr lists over 140 charter companies with a combined fleet of more than 3,000 boats. Another useful site for online booking is www.charter.hr.

There are 50 marinas spread out along the coast, many of them operated by ACI Club (www.aci-club.hr). As well as mooring, repair facilities, water, power and fuel, most have a range of other amenities including showers, laundry, restaurants and shops. The following is a list of some of the more popular marinas, arranged from north to south.

Istria and Kvarner

Umag
☎ 052 741066

Poreč
☎ 052 451913

Vrsar
☎ 052 441052

Rovinj
☎ 052 813133

Pula
☎ 052 219142

Opatija
☎ 051 704004

Cres
☎ 051 571622

Rab
☎ 051 724023

Dalmatia
Zadar
☎ 023 332700

Kornati
☎ 023 383800

Murter
☎ 022 434411

Trogir
☎ 021 881544

Kaštela, Split
☎ 021 204010

Split
☎ 021 398548

Milna, Brač
☎ 021 636306

Palmižana, Hvar
☎ 021 744995

Korčula
☎ 020 711661

Dubrovnik
☎ 020 455020

Windsurfing
Windsurf boards can be hired in summer at all the main resorts, but the top destinations for surfers are Bol on the island of Brač and Viganj on the Pelješac Peninsula, in a narrow channel between the mainland and Korčula. Other good spots include the Premantura Peninsula, south of Pula, and Krk out in Kvarner bay.

What's On When

Carnival in Lastovo

Croatia's most unusual Carnival celebration takes place on the remote island of Lastovo each Shrove Tuesday, when a straw figure known as Poklad is paraded through town on a donkey and attached to a rope while fireworks are let off beneath his feet. At the end of the procession, the Poklad is ritually burnt while villagers in red shirts and black waistcoats perform a local variation of the Moreška sword dance.

Every town and city in Croatia has its own annual feast day, held in honour of the patron saint or to commemorate a historic victory over the Turks. The celebrations are usually a mix of religious and secular, with processions, Masses, fireworks, music, dancing and crowds in traditional folk costume. In Slavonia, you will see people dancing the *kolo* (circle dance) to the sound of the *tamburica*, while in Dalmatia you may hear a *klapa* (male voice choir). Details are available from local tourist offices.

February/March

St Blaise (3 February):

Large procession in Dubrovnik in honour of the city's patron saint, whose relics are carried around the old town.

Carnival (February/March):

The pre-Lenten Carnival is celebrated across the country, though the biggest parade takes place in Rijeka on the Sunday before Shrove Tuesday.

March/April

Good Friday:

Religious processions in Korčula and in the villages around Jelsa on Hvar.

St Vincent (28 April):

The Kumpanija sword dance is performed in the village of Blato on Korčula.

May

St Domnius (7 May):

Feast day in Split in honour of the patron saint.

Rab Tournament (9 May):

Re-enactment of a medieval tournament in Rab, in which knights fight each other with crossbows.

July

Ðakovski Vekovi (first weekend):

'Ðakovo Embroidery' is a celebration of Slavonian folk culture, with *tamburica* music, dancing and displays of gypsy wagons and horses.

Rab Tournament (27 July):

Re-enactment of a medieval tournament in Rab, in which knights fight each other with crossbows.

St Theodor (29 July):

Performances of the Moreška sword dance (► 111) in Korčula.

August

Sinjska Alka (first Sunday):

Medieval jousting by horsemen in cavalry uniform in the Dalmatian town of Sinj.

Trka Na Prstenac (mid-August):

Displays of horsemanship at the 'Tilting at the Ring' festival in the Istrian town of Barban.

Assumption (15 August):

Large pilgrimage to Marija Bistrica. Another takes place on 8 September to mark the birth of the Virgin.

September

St Euphemia (16 September):

Feast day in Rovinj in honour of the patron saint.

Practical Matters

*Above: the good life in
Rovinj old town*

TIME DIFFERENCES

GMT	Croatia	Germany	USA (NY)
12 noon	1PM	1PM	7AM

BEFORE YOU GO

WHAT YOU NEED

		UK & Ireland	USA & Canada	Australia	New Zealand	EU Countries
●	Required					
○	Suggested					
▲	Not required	Some countries require a passport to remain valid for a minimum period (usually at least six months) beyond the date of entry—contact their consulate or embassy or your travel agent for details.				
Passport or National Identity Card where applicable		●	●	●	●	●
Visa		▲	▲	▲	▲	▲
Onward or return ticket		○	○	○	○	○
Health inoculations		▲	▲	▲	▲	▲
Health documentation (▶ 123, Health)		▲	▲	▲	▲	▲
Travel insurance		○	○	○	○	○
Driving licence (national with Italian translation or international)		●	●	●	●	●
Car insurance certificate (if own car)		●	●	●	●	●
Car registration document (if own car)		●	●	●	●	●

WHEN TO GO

Dubrovnik

High season

Low season

11°C	12°C	14°C	17°C	21°C	25°C	28°C	28°C	25°C	21°C	16°C	13°C
JAN	FEB	MAR	APR	MAY	JUN	JUL	AUG	SEP	OCT	NOV	DEC

🌦 Wet   ☁ Cloud   ☀ Sun   🌦 Sunshine/Showers

TOURIST OFFICES

In the UK
Croatian National Tourist Office
2 The Lanchesters,
162–164 Fulham Palace Road,
London, W6 9ER
☎ 020 8563 7979

In the US
Croatian National Tourist Office
350 Fifth Avenue
Suite 4003
New York, NY 10118
☎ 212 279 8672 or toll-free on 800 829 4416

On the Web
Tourist information on Croatia is available in Croatian, English and German on the Croatian National Tourist Board website at
www.croatia.hr.

NATIONAL POLICE 92

FIRE 93

AMBULANCE 94

WHEN YOU ARE THERE

ARRIVING

There are international airports at Dubrovnik, Zagreb, Split, Pula, Rijeka and Zadar. Croatia Airlines operates flights to Zagreb from most major European capitals. Ferries from Italy arrive at Zadar, Split and Dubrovnik, with services to Istria and to the main islands in summer. Buses and trains from central Europe arrive in Zagreb. You can drive into Croatia from Slovenia, Hungary, Bosnia-Herzegovina and Serbia and Montenegro.

Zagreb (Pleso) Airport Distance to city centre	Journey times
17km	📱 N/A
	🚌 30 minutes
	🚗 15 minutes CAR

Dubrovnik (Gruž) Harbour Distance to city centre	Journey times
3km	📱 N/A
	🚌 10 minutes
	🚗 10 minutes CAR

MONEY

Croatia's currency is the kuna (kn), which is divided into 100 lipa. Coins are issued in denominations of 1, 2, 5, 10, 20 and 50 lipa, 1kn, 2kn and 5kn. Notes are issued in denominations of 5, 10, 20, 50, 100, 200, 500 and 1,000kn. The euro is widely accepted and many prices are quoted in both euros and kuna. Credit cards are widely used. You can withdraw money from ATM (cashpoint) machines using a credit or debit card with a PIN (personal identification number).

TIME

 Croatia is on Central European Time, one hour ahead of Greenwich Mean Time. Summer time (GMT+2) operates from the last Sunday in March to the last Sunday in October.

CUSTOMS

 YES

200 cigarettes OR 50 cigars OR 250g of tobacco
1 litre of spirits
2 litres of sparkling or dessert wines
2 litres of wine
50ml of perfume
250ml of toilet water
1kg of coffee

Travellers under 18 years of age are not entitled to the tobacco and alcohol allowances.

Any amount of foreign currency may be imported to Croatia. The limit on importing or exporting Croatian currency is 15,000kn.

Pets may only be brought into Croatia if accompanied by an International Vaccination Certificate.

Valuable photographic and computer equipment should be declared at the border.

 NO

Drugs, firearms, ammunition, offensive weapons, obscene material, unlicensed animals.

CONSULATES

USA
01 661 220

UK
01 600 9100

Germany
01 630 0100

Ireland
01 667 4455

WHEN YOU ARE THERE

TOURIST OFFICES

TOURIST OFFICES
- Zagreb
  Trg Bana Jelačića 11
  ☎ 01 481 4051
  www.zagreb-touristinfo.hr
- Dubrovnik
  Stradun ☎ 020 321561
  www.tzdubrovnik.hr
- Hvar
  Trg Svetog Stjepana
  ☎ 021 741059
  www.hvar.hr
- Poreč
  Zagrebačka 9
  ☎ 052 451293
  www.istra.com/porec
- Pula
  Forum 3 ☎ 052 212987
  www.pulainfo.hr
- Rovinj
  Obala Pina Budicina 12
  ☎ 052 811566
  www.tzgrovinj.hr
- Split
  Peristil ☎ 021 345606
  www.visitsplit.com

There are tourist information offices in all main towns and resorts, though some are only open in summer, particularly on the islands. Staff are multi-lingual and can generally issue free maps and guides. Local travel agencies such as Atlas have offices in all the main towns and are good sources of information and private rooms.

Tourist information in English, German and Italian is available on a dedicated telephone number throughout Croatia from April to October. Call Croatian Angels (☎ 062 999999).

NATIONAL HOLIDAYS

J	F	M	A	M	J	J	A	S	O	N	D
2		(1)		1(1)			1			1	3

1 Jan	New Year's Day
6 Jan	Epiphany
Mar/Apr	Easter Monday
1 May	Labour Day
May/Jun	Corpus Christi
22 Jun	Anti-Fascist Resistance Day
25 Jun	Croatian National Day
5 Aug	Victory Day
15 Aug	Feast of the Assumption
8 Oct	Independence Day
1 Nov	All Saints' Day
25-26 Dec	Christmas

OPENING HOURS

○ Shops   ● Main Post Offices
● Offices   ● Pharmacies
● Banks   ● Museums

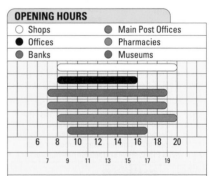

Most shops are closed on Saturday afternoon and all day Sunday. Some shops close for a break on weekday afternoons. Shopping centres in Zagreb, and shops in coastal resorts in summer, may stay open for longer hours and on Sundays. Banks and post offices are generally open on Saturday mornings. In larger towns, there will usually be a duty pharmacy open at night and weekends. Museums are generally closed on Mondays and on weekend after-noons.

DRIVE ON THE RIGHT

TOILETS CHEAP

Not many public toilets. Use cafés instead.

PUBLIC TRANSPORT

Buses
Buses are generally the easiest way to get around, with an extensive network of services connecting the main towns, cities and resorts. In big cities such as Zagreb, you should buy your ticket in advance from the ticket windows at the main bus station. On local and island routes, you can buy your ticket on the bus.

Trains
The rail network covers most major cities with the exception of Dubrovnik. High-speed tilting trains, equipped with personal headphones and laptop connections, were introduced in 2004 on the route from Zagreb to Split, reducing the journey time to five hours.

Urban Transport
The larger cities such as Zagreb, Split and Dubrovnik have their own municipal bus services. Tickets are available from the driver but are cheaper if bought in advance from newspaper kiosks. Zagreb also has an efficient network of trams, and a funicular railway between the upper and lower towns. The Zagreb Card, available from tourist offices, gives free access to public transport for 72 hours.

Ferries
Car and passenger ferries between islands and the mainland are operated by Jadrolinija. There is also a daily car ferry along the Adriatic coast from Rijeka to Dubrovnik, stopping at Zadar, Split, Hvar, Korčula and Mljet. There is no system of reservations for local ferries, so you should arrive at the harbour well in advance, particularly if you are travelling by car. Timetables and fares are available at all ferry ports or at **www.**jadrolinija.hr.

CAR RENTAL

The leading international car rental companies have offices at the main airports. There are also local companies in all major resorts. Keep your hire documents, passport and driving licence with you at all times, and never leave them unattended in the car.

TAXIS

Taxis can be hired from cab ranks in Zagreb and other main towns. Taxi ranks can usually be found at bus and train stations and ferry ports. Fares are metered, with supplements for late-night travel and at weekends, and an additional charge payable for luggage.

DRIVING

Speed limit on motorways (*autocesta*—toll payable): **130kph** (80mph)

Speed limit on main roads: **110kph** (68mph) (minor roads **90kph/56mph**)

Speed limit on urban roads: **50kph** (30mph)

Seat belts must be worn at all times. Children under 12 must sit in the back seat.

The use of mobile phones while driving is forbidden.

Headlights must be switched on at all times.

The drink-drive limit is zero and is strictly enforced.

Fuel is sold in various grades, including Eurosuper 95, Super 98 and Eurodiesel. Petrol stations are usually open from 7am–8pm (7am–10pm in summer), though on motorways and major roads they are open 24 hours.

If you are driving your own car in Croatia, you should take out European breakdown cover before you leave. Roadside assistance is provided by the Hrvatski Autoklub (+ 987) according to a fixed scale of charges. Car hire firms will provide their own rescue service.

PERSONAL SAFETY

Violence against tourists is unusual. Theft from cars is the most common form of crime.
• Do not leave valuables on the beach or poolside.
• Always lock valuables in hotel safety deposit boxes.
• Never leave anything inside your car. If you have to, lock it out of sight in the boot.
• Beware of pickpockets in crowded markets, and on buses and trams in Dubrovnik, Split and Zagreb.

Police assistance:
☎ **+92 from any phone**

TELEPHONES

There are public telephones in all main towns and resorts. Phonecards (*telefonska kartica*) can be bought at post offices, news kiosks and shops displaying the HT (Hrvatski Telekom) logo. Mobile phone coverage is almost universal; make sure your phone is switched to international roaming before you go. The international dialling code for Croatia is 385.

International Dialling Codes

from Croatia to:

UK:	00 44
USA/Canada:	00 1
Ireland:	00 353
Australia:	00 61

POST

Main post offices are open from Monday to Friday 7am–7pm, and on Saturday mornings. In smaller towns and on islands, they may be open on weekday mornings only. The post office next to the railway station in Zagreb is open 24 hours. Stamps can be bought at post offices and news kiosks.

ELECTRICITY

The power supply is 220 volts AC. Sockets take two-pronged round continental plugs. Visitors from the UK will need an adaptor and visitors from the USA will require a transformer for appliances operating on 100–120 volts.

TIPS/GRATUITIES

Tipping is not expected for all services and rates are generally lower than elsewhere.

Yes ✓   No ✗

Restaurants	✓	10%
Cafés/bars	✓	change
Taxis	✓	10%
Tour guides	✓	10-20kn
Chambermaids	✓	10-20kn
Porters	✓	10kn
Toilets	✗	

PHOTOGRAPHY

What to photograph: coastline, islands, national parks, Croatian towns, people.

Best time to photograph: early morning and evening, when the sunlight is subtle rather than overpowering.

Where to buy film: film and camera batteries are widely available at newsagents, kiosks and supermarkets.

HEALTH

Insurance Citizens of European Union countries receive free emergency medical treatment on production of their passport. This covers essential hospital stays but excludes some expenses such as the cost of prescribed medicines. Private medical insurance is still advised and is essential for all other visitors.

Dental Services Dental treatment has to be paid for by all visitors but is usually covered by private medical insurance.

Sun Advice The sun is intense on the Adriatic coast in summer and it is possible to burn very quickly. Cover up with a high-factor sunscreen, wear a hat and drink plenty of water. Children are especially vulnerable and need to be protected, especially when playing near the sea.

Drugs Prescription and non-prescription drugs and medicines are available from pharmacies (*ljekarna*). Outside normal hours, a notice on the door of each pharmacy should give the address of the nearest duty chemist. Take adequate supplies of any drugs that you need regularly as they may not be available. Other items to consider include insect repellent, anti-diarrhoea pills and sea-sickness tablets.

Safe Water Tap water is safe to drink. Bottled mineral water is widely available.

CONCESSIONS

Students

Holders of an International Student Identity Card (ISIC) may be able to obtain discounts on public transport and entrance fees. There are youth hostels in Zagreb, Pula, Zadar and Dubrovnik, with discounts for students, people under 26 and members of hostelling organisations (see **www.hfhs.hr**).

Senior Citizens

Travellers over 60 are generally entitled to reduced fares on public transport and reduced entrance fees at museums.

Children

Children under 12 travel half-price on most buses, trains and ferries, while children under three travel free of charge.

CLOTHING SIZES

USA	UK	Croatia/Europe	
36	36	46	
38	38	48	
40	40	50	Suits
42	42	52	
44	44	54	
46	46	56	
8	7	41	
8.5	7.5	42	
9.5	8.5	43	Shoes
10.5	9.5	44	
11.5	10.5	45	
12	11	46	
14.5	14.5	37	
15	15	38	
15.5	15.5	39/40	Shirts
16	16	41	
16.5	16.5	42	
17	17	43	
6	8	34	
8	10	36	
10	12	38	Dresses
12	14	40	
14	16	42	
16	18	44	
6	4.5	38	
6.5	5	38	
7	5.5	39	Shoes
7.5	6	39	
8	6.5	40	
8.5	7	41	

WHEN DEPARTING

- Contact the airport on the day before leaving to ensure the flight details are unchanged.
- The airport departure tax, payable when you leave Croatia, is already included in the cost of the airline ticket.

LANGUAGE

The official language of Croatia is Croatian (*hrvatski*). Until 1991 this was known as Serbo-Croat but it is now recognized as a separate language. Unlike Serbian, which uses the Cyrillic script, Croatian uses the Latin alphabet, though otherwise many words are identical. Croatian is entirely phonetic, which means that every word is pronounced exactly as it is written. Additional letters used in Croatian are č (pronounced 'ch'), ć (almost the same), š (pronouned 'sh'), ž (pronounced like a 'j') and đ (pronouned 'dj'). The letter 'c' is pronounced 'ts'.

	hotel	*hotel*	telephone	*telefon*
	rooms	*sobe*	television	*televizor*
	apartment	*apartman*	breakfast	*doručak*
	bath	*kupaona*	half-board	*polupansion*
	shower	*tuš*	key	*ključ*
	toilet	*zahod*	reservation	*rezervacija*
	balcony	*balkon*	campsite	*autokamp*
	bank	*banka*	stamp	*poštanske marka*
	exchange	*mjenjacnica*	postcard	*razglednica*
	cashier	*blagajnik*	cheap	*jeftino*
	money	*novac*	expensive	*skupo*
	credit card	*kreditna karta*	open	*otvoreno*
	post office	*pošta*	closed	*zatvoreno*
	restaurant	*restauracija*	beer	*pivo*
	café	*kavana*	wine	*vino*
	cake shop	*slastičarnica*	coffee	*kava*
	lunch	*ručak*	tea	*čaj*
	dinner	*večeru*	ice-cream	*sladoled*
	bread	*kruh*	fish	*riba*
	water	*voda*	the bill	*račun*
	bus	*autobus*	ferry	*trajekt*
	tram	*tramvaj*	ticket	*karta*
	train	*vlak*	timetable	*vozni red*
	bus station	*autobusna stanica*	arrival	*dolazak*
	train station	*zeljeznički kolodvor*	departure	*odlazak*
			entrance	*ulaz*
			exit	*izlaz*
	airport	*zračna luka*	taxi	*taksi*
	port	*luka*	petrol	*benzin*
	hi	*bok*	here you are	*izvolite*
	hello/good day	*dobar dan*	cheers!	*¡ivjeli!*
	good morning	*dobro jutro*	large	*velik*
	good evening	*dobra večer*	small	*malen*
	goodbye	*doviđenj*	Croatia	*hrvatska*
	please	*molim*	America	*amerika*
	thank you	*hvala*	England	*engleska*
	excuse me	*oprostite*	I don't understand	*ne razumijem*
	go away!	*odlazi!*		
	yes	*da*	do you speak English?	*govorite li engleski*
	no	*ne*		

INDEX

INDEX

Acknowledgements

The Automobile Association wishes to thank the following photographers and libraries and associations for their assistance in the preparation of this book:

Yevgeny Khaldei/CORBIS 10; Reuters/CORBIS 11t, 11c; NIKOLA SOLIC/Reuters/Corbis 11b; Getty Images 14b; Miriam Reik/Alamy 20; WWW.GENERALIC.COM 36r, 37l

The remaining photographs are held in the Association's own photo library (**AA PHOTO LIBRARY**) and were taken by PETE BENNETT.

Page layout: Katherine Mead and Nick Otway   **Indexer:** Marie Lorimer

Dear Essential Traveller

Your comments, opinions and recommendations are very important to us. So please help us to improve our travel guides by taking a few minutes to complete this simple questionnaire.

You do not need a stamp (unless posted outside the UK). If you do not want to cut this page from your guide, then photocopy it or write your answers on a plain sheet of paper.

Send to: **The Editor, AA World Travel Guides, FREEPOST SCE 4598, Basingstoke RG21 4GY.**

Your recommendations…

We always encourage readers' recommendations for restaurants, nightlife or shopping – if your recommendation is used in the next edition of the guide, we will send you a *FREE* AA *Essential* **Guide** of your choice. Please state below the establishment name, location and your reasons for recommending it.

_____

_____

_____

_____

Please send me **AA *Essential*** _____

About this guide…

Which title did you buy?

　　AA *Essential* _____

Where did you buy it? _____

When? m m / y y

Why did you choose an AA *Essential* Guide? _____

_____

_____

_____

_____

Did this guide meet your expectations?

　　Exceeded ☐　Met all ☐　Met most ☐　Fell below ☐

　　Please give your reasons_____

_____

_____

_____

continued on next page…

Were there any aspects of this guide that you particularly liked? ________

____

____

Is there anything we could have done better? ________

____

____

About you...

Name (*Mr/Mrs/Ms*) ________

Address ________

____

________ Postcode ________

Daytime tel nos ________

Please only give us your mobile phone number if you wish to hear from us about other products and services from the AA and partners by text or mms.

Which age group are you in?

Under 25 ☐ 25–34 ☐ 35–44 ☐ 45–54 ☐ 55–64 ☐ 65+ ☐

How many trips do you make a year?

Less than one ☐ One ☐ Two ☐ Three or more ☐

Are you an AA member? Yes ☐ No ☐

About your trip...

When did you book? m m / y y When did you travel? m m / y y

How long did you stay? ________

Was it for business or leisure? ________

Did you buy any other travel guides for your trip?

If yes, which ones? ________

Thank you for taking the time to complete this questionnaire. Please send it to us as soon as possible, and remember, you do not need a stamp (*unless posted outside the UK*).

Happy Holidays!

The information we hold about you will be used to provide the products and services requested and for identification, account administration, analysis, and fraud/loss prevention purposes. More details about how that information is used is in our privacy statement, which you'll find under the heading "Personal Information" in our terms and conditions and on our website: www.theAA.com. Copies are also available from us by post, by contacting the Data Protection Manager at AA, Southwood East, Apollo Rise, Farnborough, Hampshire GU14 OJW.

We may want to contact you about other products and services provided by us, or our partners (by mail, telephone) but please tick the box if you DO NOT wish to hear about such products and services from us by mail or telephone. ☐

The Atlas

Pete Bennett: *Our Lady of the Snows, Marija Bistrica*

Day One

Day Two

Day Three

Day Four

Day Five

Day Six

Day Seven

www.theAA.com
The Automobile Association's website offers comprehensive and up-to-the-minute information covering AA-approved hotels, guest houses and B&Bs, restaurants and pubs in the UK; airport parking, insurance, European breakdown cover, European motoring advice, a ferry planner, European route planner, overseas fuel prices, a bookshop and much more.

The Foreign and Commonwealth Office
www.fco.gov.uk
Country advice, traveller's tips, before you go information, checklists and more.

Croatian National Tourist Board
www.croatia.hr
Croatia's official website, with information in Croatian, English and German.

GENERAL

UK Passport Service
www.ukpa.gov.uk

US Passport Information
www.travel.state.gov

Health Advice for Travellers
www.doh.gov.uk/traveladvice

BBC – Holiday
www.bbc.co.uk/holiday

The Full Universal Currency Converter
www.xe.com/ucc/full.shtml

www.hr
Croatian homepage, with thousands of links in Croatian and English.

www.mvp.hr
Official site of the Ministry of Foreign Affairs—includes visa information.

www.hina.hr
News agency with the latest news from Croatia in Croatian and English.

www.cronatur.com
Comprehensive advice for naturists visiting Croatia.

www.inyourpocket.com/zagreb
Up-to-date listings of bars, clubs, restaurants and shops in Zagreb.

www.zagreb-touristinfo.hr
Official site of the Zagreb Tourist Board.

www.istra.hr
Official site of the Istria Tourist Board.

www.visitdubrovnik.hr
Information on Dubrovnik and the surrounding area.

TRAVEL

Croatia Airlines
www.croatiaairlines.hr

Croatian Ferries
www.adrolinija.hr

Croatian Railways
www.hznet.hr

European Rail
www.europeanrail.com

Flying with Kids
www.flyingwithkids.com

Motorway

National road

Regional road

Local road

Other road

International boundary

City

Town

National park

Place of interest

Airport

1831 Height in metres

0   50 km

0   30 miles

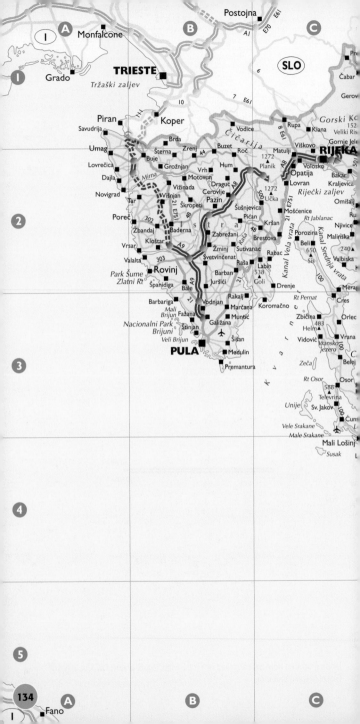

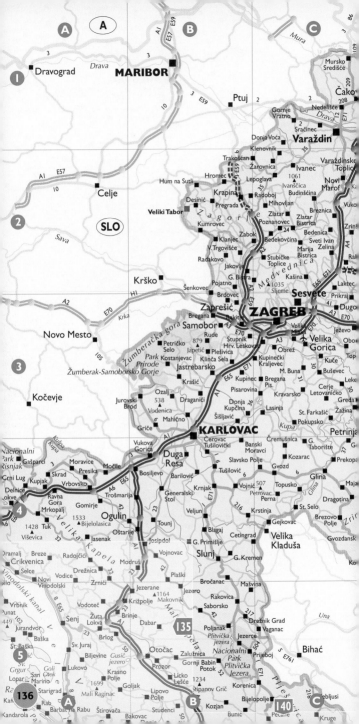

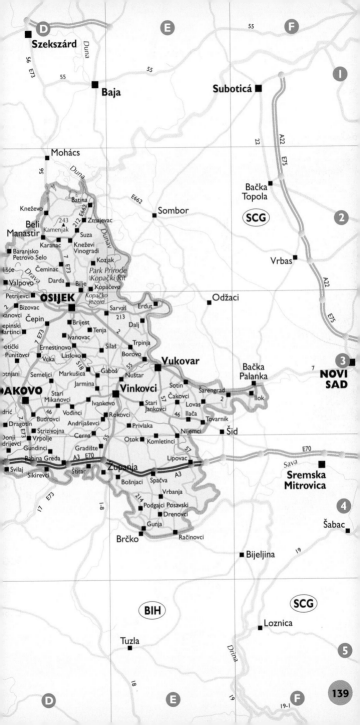

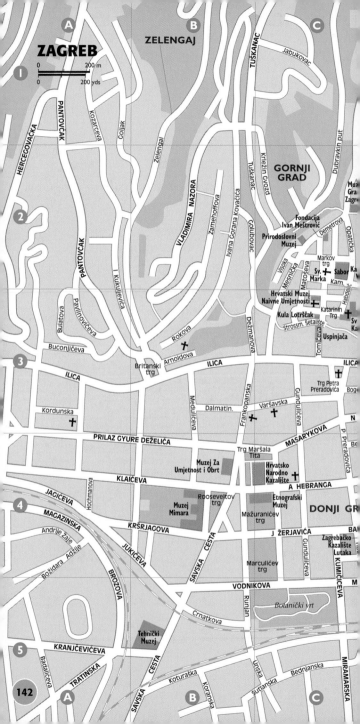

ZAGREB

ZELENGAJ

GORNJI GRAD

Mu×
Gra
Zagr

Fondacija
Ivan Meštrović

Prirodoslovni
Muzej

Markov
trg

Sv. ☩ Sabor   Ka
Marka

Kam

Hrvatski Muzej
Naivne Umjetnosti ☩

Kula Lotrščak

Katarinin
trg ☩ Sv
Ka

Strossm. Šetalište

Uspinjača

Britanski
trg ☩

ILICA

ILICA

ILICA

Trg Petra
Preradovića ☩

Bog

Kordunska ☩

PRILAZ GYURE DEŽELIĆA

Dalmatin.   Varšavska

☩   ☩

MASARYKOVA

p Preradovića

Be

N

Trg Maršala
Tita

Muzej Za
Umjetnost i Obrt

Hrvatsko
Narodno
Kazalište ☩

A HEBRANGA

DONJI GR

JAGIĆEVA

MAGAZINSKA

KLAIĆEVA

Rooseveljtov
trg

Muzej
Mimara

KRŠRJAGOVA

Etnografski
Muzej

Mažuranićev
trg

BA

Zagrebačko
Kazalište
Lutaka

Andrije žale

JUKIĆEVA

BROZOVA

SAVSKA CESTA

J ŽERJAVIĆA

Marculićev
trg

VODNIKOVA

Crnatkova

Runjan

Botanički vrt

Tehnički
Muzej

KRANJČEVIĆEVA

SAVSKA CESTA

Koturaška

Unska

Bednjanska

MIRAMARSKA

TRATINSKA

A   B   C

0   200 m
0   200 yds

For the main index see pages 125–126